D1527411

Benjamin Britten

COMPOSER RESOURCE MANUALS
VOLUME 39
GARLAND REFERENCE LIBRARY OF THE HUMANITIES
VOLUME 1867

COMPOSER RESOURCE MANUALS
GUY A. MARCO, *General Editor*

STEPHEN COLLINS FOSTER
A Guide to Research
by Calvin Elliker

JOHANNES OCKEGHEM
AND JACOB OBRECHT
A Guide to Research
by Martin Picker

ALESSANDRO AND
DOMENICO SCARLATTI
A Guide to Research
by Carole F. Vidali

CLAUDIO MONTEVERDI
A Guide to Research
by K. Gary Adams
and Dyke Kiel

CARL MARIA VON WEBER
A Guide to Research
by Donald G. Henderson
and Alice H. Henderson

GIOVANNI BATTISTA PERGOLESI
A Guide to Research
by Marvin E. Paymer
and Hermine W. Williams

CLAUDE DEBUSSY
A Guide to Research
by James Briscoe

FRANZ JOSEPH HAYDN
A Guide to Research
by Floyd K. Grave
and Margaret G. Grave

HENRY PURCELL
A Guide to Research
by Franklin B. Zimmerman

GUILLAUME DE MACHAUT
A Guide to Research
by Lawrence Earp

EDWARD ELGAR
A Guide to Research
by Christopher Kent

BENJAMIN BRITTEN
A Guide to Research
by Peter J. Hodgson

ALBAN BERG
A Guide to Research
by Bryan R. Simms

BENJAMIN BRITTEN
A GUIDE TO RESEARCH

PETER J. HODGSON

GARLAND PUBLISHING, INC.
NEW YORK AND LONDON
1996

Library of Congress Cataloging-in-Publication Data

Hodgson, Peter John, 1929–
    Benjamin Britten : a guide to research / Peter J. Hodgson.
        p.   cm. — (Garland reference library of the humanities ; vol.
1867) (Composer resource manuals ; v. 39)
    Includes index.
    ISBN 0-8153-1795-6 (alk. paper)
    1. Britten, Benjamin, 1913–1976—Bibliography.   I. Title.   II. Series.
III. Series: Garland composer resource manuals ; v. 39.
    ML134.B85H63   1996
    016.78'092—dc20   96–19632
                                               CIP
                                              MN

Printed on acid-free, 250-year-life paper
Manufactured in the United States of America

COMPOSER RESOURCE MANUALS

In response to the growing need for bibliographic guidance to the vast literature on significant composers, Garland is publishing an extensive series of research guides. This ongoing series encompasses more than 50 composers; they represent Western musical tradition from the Renaissance to the present century.

Each research guide offers a selective, annotated list of writings, in all European languages, about one or more composers. There are also lists of works by the composers, unless these are available elsewhere. Biographical sketches and guides to library resources, organizations, and specialists are presented. As appropriate to the individual composer, there are maps, photographs, or other illustrative matter, glossaries, and indexes.

To Mary
for her patience.

CONTENTS

PREFACE

Benjamin Britten attracted international attention and his music was a focus of interest for a large number of performers and scholars, as well as amateurs, during the composer's lifetime. That interest has not diminished since his death in 1976. On the contrary, study of Britten and his music has continued to expand significantly over the past two decades.

This Composer Resource Manual is intended to serve as a concise, introductory guide for those who wish to explore aspects of Britten's life and music. Drawing upon the literature of more than half a century, it provides brief background notes on the composer, an inventory of his music, and a select bibliography with annotations.

A Britten Source Book (Evans/Reed/Wilson, 1987) is recognized for its pioneering work in the field of Britten studies, for its wealth of detail, and for its inspiration in the compilation of this Composer Resource Manual on Benjamin Britten. While this manual seeks neither to complement nor to supplement the earlier source book, there are some correlations between the two studies, especially in the area of bibliography where *A Britten Source Book* covers the field with more than 3,000 citations. Although designed as an independent reference guide to the literature on and about the life and music of Benjamin Britten, some repetition of detail found in *A Britten Source Book* proved unavoidable in this Composer Resource Manual. Neither book, however, makes the other redundant and, whenever appropriate, a reference to *A Britten Source Book* has been preferred to unnecessary duplication of information in this manual.

ACKNOWLEDGMENTS

Many friends contributed to the work on this Composer Resource Manual. Research begun in 1986 at Texas Christian University was assisted by music librarian Sheila Madden. After 1987, the project continued at Principia College with help from several departments. Marsha Burruss Ballard, Susan Fuller, David Haslam, and Daphne Selbert in the Marshall Brooks Library were unstinting in their support, as were many other colleagues on the campus. An academic leave and a grant from Principia College in the spring of 1995 added impetus to the research. Fred Hunter, my friend in London, was a source of stimulating information from the beginning of the project to its completion.

Britten-Pears Library staff were invariably encouraging and provided prompt assistance during and between my visits to the Library in 1987 and again in 1995. Helen Risdon, Sylvia Rush, and Pamela Wheeler graciously responded to my queries and were most helpful in locating items of interest. I am deeply indebted to Paul Banks for permission to use materials furnished by the Library.

Andrea Lawrenz and **Marie Oleson** deserve special thanks for providing me with considerable technical assistance and support. Without their generous and timely aid the project would doubtless have languished.

Peter J. Hodgson

Principia College
Elsah, Illinois

PART I

NOTES

This part is intended as background for Parts II and III. It contains introductory notes on Benjamin Britten, The Britten-Pears Library, and related items of interest.

Biographical notes

Birth	22 November 1913 (celebrated as the day of music's patron Saint Cecilia); 21 Kirkley Cliff Road, Lowestoft, Suffolk, England;
Christened	Edward Benjamin, 21 January 1914, St. John the Evangelist, Church of England;
Parents	Edith Rhonda (*née* Hockey) (1872-1937); Robert Victor Britten (1877-1934);
Siblings	Barbara (1902-1982); Robert (1907-1987); Elizabeth (1909-1989).

Born eight months before the outbreak of World War I (4.viii.14), Britten was almost five when it concluded (11.xi.18). His exposure to the effects of war came early. One of the first, non-musical sounds he recalled hearing was a bomb exploding in a nearby field during a German zeppelin raid in April, 1916. Lowestoft, a British naval base during World War I, is situated on the most salient seaward point of East Anglia, 20 or so miles north of Aldeburgh, also on the coast, where Britten was later to take up residence and pursue his multi-faceted musical career.

Twenty-two Kirkley Cliff Road remained the parental home
until Britten was in his early twenties when, shortly after the
death of his father in 1934, Britten's mother moved to
Frinton where she resided until her decease in the winter of
1937.

Early influences

Mrs Britten. An energetic musical amateur with a sweet
voice and some pianistic ability, Britten's mother was a
powerful early influence. She sang frequently, especially at
private gatherings in the family home where distinguished
guests (e.g., soloists with the Lowestoft Choral Society of
which Mrs Britten was secretary) also gathered and were
entertained. Britten's exposure to this home music-making
during his infancy and his participation from earliest
childhood in family theatricals as 'composer-in-residence,' as
well as accompanist to his mother who, in fact, gave her son
his first music lessons on the piano, provided the nurturing
environment essential to the development of his natural
musical abilities or what most observers refer to as 'his
genius.'

The first fruits of this indigenous development and of his
plainly precocious talent are evident in Britten's early
attempts at composition. At age five he presented his mother
with a sketch of some musical idea (unplayable!) which, in
later years, Britten acknowledged resembled more a diagram
of the Firth of Fourth Bridge than a piece of music. Quite
playable music for piano, voice, and various instrumental
combinations soon followed, however, and his juvenilia
period reflects an extraordinarily fertile musical mind,
culminating before his fifteenth birthday in such works as the
posthumously published *Quatre chansons françaises.*

THE RED HOUSE, ALDEBURGH, SUFFOLK.

23rd June, 1958.

Dear Mr. Hemmings,

I am sorry about the delay in replying to your letter, but we have been very occupied with the Aldeburgh Festival this last week.

I am afraid the Mazurka is filled with misprints owing to the haste with which it was first published.

P. 14   Line 1, bar 5, A sharp should be A natural.

"   "   Line 2, bar 5, Octave E should be E flat.

P. 8   Piano 2, 2nd note last bar, F sharp not
                                          D sharp.

P. 9   Piano 2, R.H?, end of bar 1 and beginning
          of bar 2 should be 8ve.

There may be other misprints, but these are all I can remember at the moment.

I am sorry about the recording of the Spring Symphony. It was sheduled for this year, but has had to be postponed, and I cannot say at the moment when it will be made.   Please give the boys my best wishes for the House Music Competition.

Yours sincerely,

[signature: Benjamin Britten]

Alan Hemmings Esq.,
Clifton College,
Bristol 8.

Letter typed and signed by Britten (in author's possession).

Ethel Astle (1876-1952). A second childhood influence was that of Britten's first professsional music teacher, Ethel M.K. Astle. An Associate of the Royal College of Music and a reputable local teacher, "Miss Ethel" (a form of address that was born both of familiarity and respect—her senior sister being correctly referred to as "Miss Astle") taught him music (piano, theory, transposition, and some harmony), from age seven to about fourteen. During these formative years, Britten passed the piano and theory examinations of the Associated Board of the Royal Schools of Music, including the Final level with honors a few weeks after his twelfth birthday (*Lowestoft Journal*, 23.i.26).

Ethel Astle lived with her sister and mother in the vicinity of the Britten home and conducted a pre-preparatory school which Benjamin and his siblings attended. Miss Ethel also accompanied Mrs Britten's vocal performances. It is probable that the composer's early musical activities were brought to Ethel Astle's attention and that she may have given him some simple advice, if not elementary instruction, before Britten began regular music lessons with her in 1921 at his age of seven. That Britten continued to compose with complete freedom and with growing energy and invention throughout his years of study with Miss Ethel would suggest that her influence on his creative development was, at the least, encouraging. Correspondence between them in later years confirms the affection and esteem in which pupil and teacher held each other and the worth Britten placed on his childhood learning under Ethel Astle's guidance and tutelage (see especially *Letters from A Life* [Mitchell, 1991] and unpublished letters in the Britten-Pears Archive, Aldeburgh). Ethel Astle's contribution to the early shaping of Britten's musical, personal and spiritual values invites further exploration and evaluation.

Inscribed *"To Miss Ethel. Everlastingly gratefully. Benjamin."*
Britten aged 16 (1930: the year he entered the RCM).
Photograph by Swaine, London, courtesy Britten-Pears Library.

Other influences on Britten's childhood and youth

Audrey Alston (1883-1966). At age ten, Britten began viola lessons with violist Audrey Alston of Norwich. Mrs Alston introduced Britten, shortly before his 14th birthday, to the composer Frank Bridge. This occurred after a performance of Bridge's *Enter Spring,* which the composer conducted at a concert given under the auspices of the Norfolk and Norwich Triennial Festival, 27.x.27. It was at an earlier Norwich Festival setting in 1924 when Britten, then still not eleven, had heard Bridge's orchestral suite, *The Sea,* and, in his words, "was knocked sideways."

Frank Bridge (1879-1941). Britten began composition studies with Bridge in late 1927 at age 14, taking lessons during school holidays, and at other times, through the summer of 1930 (when Britten entered the Royal College of Music) and beyond. The profound influence of this professionally exacting and forward-looking mentor (whose only pupil was Britten) on the young composer's musical and philosophical development is amply described in biographical studies.

Harold Samuel (1879-1937). Britten studied pianoforte with Samuel, at Bridge's urging, from 9.xi.28 to 14.iii.30.

John Ireland (1879-1962). One of Britten's examiners for admission to the Royal College of Music and subsequently his composition teacher at College.

Arthur Benjamin (1893-1960). Britten's lessons at the Royal College of Music were not always happy; however, he appeared to have enjoyed his piano studies with Benjamin whose humor and brilliance appealed to Britten.

Later influences

W.H. Auden (1907-1973). The first and, in many respects, most influential author and poet with whom Britten collaborated. Their earliest joint efforts were in the newly developing art of the documentary film; but Britten also contributed incidental music to plays and various ventures authored or organized by Auden and his compatriots, notably Christopher Isherwood (1904-1986) and Randall Swingler (1909-1967). Britten's first full-dress work for the stage, the operetta *Paul Bunyan,* set a libretto by Auden. Britten acknowledged the profound effect Auden had exerted on his (Britten's) developing sensitivity to the English language, although the poet's influence was by no means limited to this one sphere. Auden's departure from England for the USA early in 1939 was a factor in persuading Britten to do likewise, which he did in May of the same year.

Peter Pears (1910-1986). Britten's close companion and professional colleague for almost four decades, Pears was a distinguished tenor whose voice and artistry inspired much of Britten's operatic and vocal music. The two musicians performed together regularly in public, Britten serving as pianist or conductor. Pears was also a major organizing force in many of the musical ventures conceived jointly with Britten, including the Aldeburgh Festival. It is difficult to imagine Britten without Pears—both acknowledged their professional and personal inseparability and declared, at first privately, but now publicly through their published letters, their mutual indebtedness to each other as artists and private persons. A reading of the biographies of both Britten and Pears provides insight into their extraordinary relationship and its creative consequences.

Note on chronologies

Calendars of events in the life of Benjamin Britten are to be found in *The Britten Companion* (Palmer, 1984, based on a chronology compiled by Donald Mitchell and John Evans for *Benjamin Britten, 1913-1976: Pictures from a Life,* 1978), *A Britten Source Book* (Evans/Reed/Wilson, 1987), *Letters from a Life: The Selected Letters and Diaries of Benjamin Britten 1913-1976* (Mitchell/Reed, 1991), and *Britten* (Kennedy, 1993).

The summary of Britten's general and musical education provided here begins with his years at the pre-preparatory school in Lowestoft and concludes with his period of professional training in London, while the chronological synopsis commences with the year after Britten left the Royal College of Music, i.e., his twentieth year.

Educational summary

1919 (<u>ca</u>. age 5 years)
first music lessons from his mother;

enters Southolme, a pre-preparatory school,
conducted by the Astle family at
52 Kirkley Cliff Road, Lowestoft;

1921 (age 7 years)
begins regular music lessons,
including piano and theory,
with Ethel M.K. Astle, ARCM,
a principal at Southolme School and a
musician of good local repute;

1923 July (age 9 years/8 months)
leaves Southolme School,
but continues music education with
Ethel Astle;

September (age 9 years/10 months)
enters South Lodge Preparatory School,
Lowestoft, as a day pupil;

begins viola lessons with
Audrey Alston of Norwich;

1926 January (age 12 years/2 months)
passes Associated Board Grade VIII (Final)
pianoforte examination (with honors) under
Ethel Astle's tutelage;

1927 October (age 13 years/11 months)
Audrey Alston introduces Britten to
composer/violist/conductor Frank Bridge
at Norfolk and Norwich Triennial Festival;

November/December (age 14 years)
begins composition studies with Bridge;

1928 July (age 14 years/8 months)
leaves South Lodge;

September (age 14 years/10 months)
enters Gresham's School, Holt, Norfolk,
where Walter Greatorex is music master;

begins piano lessons with Harold Samuel;

1930 July (age 16 years/8 months)
leaves Gresham's School
with School Certificate;

September (age 16 years/10 months)
enters the Royal College of Music, London,
as a scholarship student, studying with
John Ireland (composition) and
Arthur Benjamin (pianoforte);

1933 December (age 20 years/1 month)
leaves the Royal College of Music
with the Associate diploma (ARCM)
in pianoforte performance.

A chronological synopsis

1934

23 February	First meets Peter Pears who, as a member of the BBC Singers, sang in the broadcast première of Britten's *A Boy Was Born;*
5 April	attends International Society of Contemporary Music, Florence, for performance of his *Phantasy, Op. 2;*
6 April	his father dies while Britten is in Italy;
16 October—29 November	uses Royal College of Music travel scholarship to tour Europe with his mother, visiting Paris, Munich, Basle, Salzburg, Vienna where he meets the conductor/writer Erwin Stein (Alban Berg, whom he wished to meet, was away);

1935

May	begins association with General Post Office Film Unit composing incidental music for documentary films;
5 July	first meets W.H. Auden at Downs School where Auden then taught;
October—November	begins association with London's Group Theatre and Left Theatre;

1936

January	secures exclusive publishing contract with Boosey & Hawkes;
February	his mother disposes of the family home in Lowestoft and moves to Frinton-on-Sea, an Essex seaside resort;
March	permanent staff appointment with GPO Film Unit;
April	attends International Society of Contemporary Music, Barcelona, for performance of *Suite, Op. 6,*
25 September	première of *Our Hunting Fathers, Op. 8* at Norwich Festival, a work of which Britten noted, "This is my opus one alright";

1937

31 January	his mother dies in London;
May	friendship with Peter Pears begins;
August	buys Old Mill, Snape, Suffolk;
27 August	*Bridge Variations* performed by Boyd Neel Orchestra at Salzburg Festival;
5 October	UK première of *Bridge Variations;*
19 November	BBC première of *On This Island;*

1938

June—
August
meets Aaron Copland in London at International Society of Contemporary Music; Copland visits Britten at Snape and encourages him to consider the USA and its opportunities for professional progress;

1939

May
Britten sails with Pears to North America—land at St. Jovite, Quebec Province, Canada, May 9;

21 August
Britten and Pears take up residence with Dr William and Mrs Elizabeth Meyers and family in Amityville, Long Island;

3 September
World War II declared;

1940

November
Britten and Pears move to the artist commune at 7 Middaugh Street, Brooklyn Heights, owned by George Davis, a journalist friend of W.H. Auden who resided there and presided over a household which included, at times, Salvador Dali, Gypsy Rose Lee, Louis MacNeice, and Golo Mann, among others;

1941

Spring   meets Colin McPhee who interests Britten in oriental music—records Balinese Ceremonial Music, transcribed by McPhee for two pianos, with McPhee;

Summer   stays with Pears at the home of piano duo Ethel Bartlett and Rae Robertson at Escondido, California;

                  notices E.M. Forster's article on George Crabbe in *The Listener* (found in bookshop in San Diego?);

September   returns with Pears to Mayer's residence at Amityville;

1942

2 January—   Serge Koussevitzky conducts
14 March   Boston Symphony orchestra in performance of *Sinfonia da Requiem;* Britten discusses idea for an opera using Crabbe's *The Borough;* Koussevitzky later tells Britten that The Koussevitzky Music Foundation (established in memory of his wife) had awarded Britten $1,000.00 to write his first opera, *Peter Grimes;*

1942

16 March—   Britten and Pears return to the UK
17 April   on a Swedish merchant ship, the
                  Axel Johnson, making the five-week
                  voyage across the Atlantic menaced
                  by Nazi U-boats, while Britten
                  composes *A Hymn to St. Cecilia,*
                  A Ceremony of Carols, and, with
                  Pears, drafts a scenario for *Peter*
                  Grimes;

17 April   Britten and Pears appear before a
                  tribunal for conscientious objectors
                  and are exempted from military
                  service, provided they perform for
                  The Council for Encouragement of
                  Music and the Arts;

1945

7 May   Allied Forces Victory in Europe;

7 June   première of *Peter Grimes* by
                  Sadler's Wells Opera Company;

1946

12 July   première of *The Rape of Lucretia*
                  at Glyndebourne Opera House;

1947

20 June   première of *Albert Herring*
                  at Glyndebourne Opera House;

1948

    5-13 June   first Aldeburgh Festival of Music and the Arts;

1951

    1 December   première of *Billy Budd* at the Royal Opera House;

1953

    8 June   première of *Gloriana* at Covent Garden;

1954

    14 September   première of *The Turn of the Screw* at Teatro La Fenice, Venice;

1957

    1 January   première of *The Prince of the Pagodas* at Covent Garden;

    8 April   American Academy of Arts and Letters and the National Institute of Arts and Letters, New York, elects Britten to membership;

    14-23 June   10th Aldeburgh Festival;

1958

    18 June   première of *Noye's Fludde* at Orford Church;

1959

| 11 June | Honorary Doctorate conferred by Cambridge University; |

1960

| 11 June | première of *A Midsummer Night's Dream;* |

1962

| 30 May | première of *War Requiem* at St. Michael's Cathedral, Coventry; |
| 22 October | Borough of Aldeburgh confers Honorary Freedom; |

1964

| 13 June | première of *Curlew River;* |
| 31 July | receives First Aspen Award; |

1965

| 23 March | awarded the Order of Merit; |
| 9 October | receives Wilhuris Sibelius Prize in Helsinki; |

1966

| 9 June | première of *The Burning Fiery Furnace;* |

1967

2-25 June	20th Aldeburgh Festival, attended by HM Queen Elizabeth II who opens The Maltings Concert Hall, Snape;
September-October	Recital tour with Pears—Montreal, New York, Mexico Peru, Chile, Argentina, Brazi;

1968

25 May	receives Sonning Prize, Copenhagen;
10 June	première of *The Prodigal Son;*

1969

January	recitals with Pears at Schloss Elmau for tenth anniversay of 'British-Deutsche Musiktage';
7 June	Maltings Concert Hall burns;

1970

June	23rd Aldeburgh Festival in rebuilt Maltings Concert Hall;

1971

16 May	broadcast première of *Owen Wingrave;*

1972

  2-19 June   25th Aldeburgh Festival;

1973

  16 June   première of *Death in Venice* at
                         The Maltings, Snape;

1974

  November   awarded the Ravel Prize;

1976

  1 February   broadcast première of
                       Paul Bunyan;

  4 June   stage première of revised
                       version of *Paul Bunyan;*

  12 June   named a Life Peer in
                       The Queen's Birthday Honours
                       List and becomes
                       Baron Britten of Aldeburgh
                       in the County of Suffolk;

  4 December   dies at home, the Red House,
                       Aldeburgh.

1986

  3 April   Peter Pears dies at home,
                       the Red House, Aldeburgh.

The Britten-Pears Library

There is no better resource for Britten studies than the centre created in Aldeburgh and named after the composer and his companion. Information concerning this centre is provided in a brief brochure obtainable from The Britten-Pears Library upon request. Descriptive detail of the Library, excerpted from this brochure, is reproduced here with permission.

Origin and location

The Britten-Pears Library was assembled over the years by Benjamin Britten and Peter Pears and is a working collection of manuscripts, books, music, and recordings reflecting their interests and activities as performing artists. To this has been added a considerable quantity of related materials. The Library is adjacent to the Red House, once a farm-house, where Benjamin Britten and Peter Pears came to live in 1957, and is housed partly in former farm buildings adapted in 1963 by Peter Collymore. The Library was greatly expanded in 1993 with the opening of an extension, designed by Robert Wilson and Malcolm Ness, providing better access, a new display area, offices, and additional air-conditioned storage for archival materials.

Access

By online catalogue. Automation of catalogue records began in 1990. By early 1995, some 28,000 records (about 20% of the collections) had been created. Since March 1995 the records in four of the Library's databases—Books and Literary Mss, Printed and Ms Music, Sound Recordings, Letters and Archives—have been accessible through the INFO System at the University of East Anglia. The UEA database, regularly updated, offers general search capabilities which complement the more focused bibliographic searches available at the Britten-Pears Library. Still under development, enhancements to search routines and displays are anticipated. For access to this catalogue:

1 Telnet library.uea.ac.uk
2 At the prompt type 'nepac'
3 At the second screen select
  the Britten-Pears Library
  from the list of catalogues.

By personal visit. The Library is open to scholars and research students by appointment only. All enquiries should be addressed in writing to:

Librarian
Britten-Pears Library
The Red House
Aldeburgh, Suffolk IP15 5PZ
England

Telephone (01144728) 452 615
Fax (01144728) 453 076
E-mail bpl@uea.ac.uk

General library

This comprises a growing collection which includes printer's copies, proofs and early editions of Britten's works; a general collection of poetry, drama and other subjects, including important source material for students of Britten's life and works; music used and annotated by Benjamin Britten or Peter Pears; English vocal music, from the sixteenth-century to the present, much of it in early editions, and literature related to English songs and singers.

General archive

This is concerned especially with the careers of Benjamin Britten and Peter Pears. Friends and colleagues of these two artists have made important contributions.

Printed ephemera. There is a large collection of programmes (including those of first performances of Britten's works) and reviews of concerts and recitals given by Pears and Britten extending over a period of a half century.

Photographs. This collection of over 12,000 items covers many aspects of the lives of Peter Pears, Benjamin Britten and their associates. The Aldeburgh Festival, from its foundation in 1948, is fully represented here.

Sound and film. The Britten-Pears Library seeks to acquire a copy of every commercially available recording of Britten's music. In addition it holds an extensive archive of sound recordings, videos and films relating to the lives of Britten and Pears, including many unique items.

Special collections. The Archive of the English Opera Group/English Music Theatre Company (1947-1981) comprises marked production scores, designs, stage plans, lighting plots, production photographs and other items.

Music manuscripts

The Library contains a unique collection of the manuscripts of Benjamin Britten's compositions, comprising the vast majority of the works written from early boyhood until his death. This includes a number of important manuscripts belonging to the national collection at the British Library which are deposited in the Britten-Pears Library on permanent loan. Also deposited in the Library is the collection of Gustav Holst's manuscripts belonging to the Holst Foundation, and major manuscripts of Frank Bridge and Michael Tippett, together with representative scores by many other twentieth-century British composers. There is a special collection of the works of C. Armstrong Gibbs.

Other papers

Letters. The Library possesses a large collection of Britten's correspondence—approximately 25,000 items. For information on the scope of this collection and extensive published reproduction of Britten's correspondence, refer to *Letters from a Life* (Mitchell/Reed, 1991). In addition, the library is a repository for the papers of Peter Pears, including some 5,000 items of correspondence.

Literary works.   Manuscripts of poems by W.H. Auden, Wilfred Owen, Edith Sitwell, and others are in the Library, as are draft librettos of several of Britten's operas by Eric Crozier, Ronald Duncan, E.M. Forster, Myfanwy Piper and William Plomer.

Observation

Britten does not want for biographers. Yet, it has been noted, there is still need for what Robin Holloway calls "the intellectual biography more broadly interpreted—'the growth of the poet's mind'—that one most urgently wants" (see attribution below).

The scope and thrust of the first two volumes of *Letters from a Life: The Selected Letters and Diaries of Benjamin Britten 1923-1945* (Mitchell/Reed, vols. I and II, 1991) suggest that this projected five-volume series will probably come closest to fulfilling such a need. (In 1995, the three remaining volumes awaited completion and publication.) Nevertheless, one might still wish for a single-volume study (which Mitchell might have written) that embraces the conceptual frame alluded to above and which responds to such questions as (again from Holloway):

> How was Britten's particular sensibility formed? Whence his aesthetic of essentiality, his insistence on technical prowess, in a land of heartiness and amatuerism? How did the Mahler/Berg nexus so important from so early receive its ideal home in this gauche product of a dowdy seaside resort and an English public school? (Robin Holloway, "Strange Victory." In: *The Times Literary Supplement,* 13.xi.92, pp. 5-6, a review of Humphrey Carpenter's *Benjamin Britten: A Biography* [1991], and Christopher Headington's *Peter Pears: A Biography* [1992].)

PART II

MUSIC

Organized in two principal sections, this inventory of Britten's published and unpublished music is intended to provide a comprehensive overview of the composer's complete oeuvre. The first section includes an alphabetized index, music with opus numbers, and a chronological conspectus of Britten's compositional activity. The second section repeats all titles, but with full citations and under several sub-classifications.

Key to abbreviations

People, places, performance organizations

BB   Benjamin Britten
PP   Peter Pears
B-P   Britten-Pears
WHA   W.H. Auden
AF   Aldeburgh Festival
AFP   Aldeburgh Festival Program Book
ECO   The English Chamber Orchestra
LPO   The Liverpool Philharmonic Orchestra
LSO   The London Symphony Orchestra
NYP   The New York Philharmonic Orchestra
CGO   Covent Garden Opera
EOG   The English Opera Group
GOH   Glyndebourne Opera House
ROH   The Royal Opera House
RCM   The Royal College of Music
WH   Wigmore Hall

Broadcasting and film organizations

BBC   British Broadcasting Corporation
CBS   Columbia Broadcasting System
NBC   National Broadcasting Corporation
GPO   General Post Office (film group)

Publishing houses

BH   Boosey & Hawkes
FMU   Faber Music
OUP   Oxford University Press
NOV   Novello
YBP   Year Book Press

Bibliography

BSB   *A Britten Source Book* (Evans/Reed/Wilson, 1987)
KBR   *Britten* (Kennedy, 1993)
MRL   *Letters from a Life: The Selected Letters and Diaries of Benjamin Britten 1913-1976* (Mitchell/Reed, 1991)
PBC   *The Britten Companion* (Palmer, 1984)
WLO   *Benjamin Britten: His Life and Operas* (White, 1983)

Performance designations

vocal

SATB, soprano, alto, tenor, bass;
c., choir/chorus; **s.**, solo/soloists;
u., unison; **v.**, voice(s)/vocal; **med.**, medium;
acc., accompanied; **un.**, unaccompanied;

instrumental

bn., bassoon; **bcn.**, bass clarinet; **cl.**, clarinet;
sax., saxophone; **ca.**, cor anglais; **ob.**, oboe; **fl.**, flute;
pic. piccolo; **hn.**, horn; **trbn.**, trombone; **trpt.**, trumpet;
hp., harp; **org.**, organ; **pf.**, pianoforte; **perc.**, percussion;
str., string(s); **str. qt.** or **qnt.**, string quartet or quintet;
vn., violin; **va.**, viola; **vc.**, violoncello; **db.**, double bass;
acc., accordion; **inst.**, instrument(s); **orch.**, orchestra;

various

arr., arranged/arrangement; **ad.**, adapted;
ed., editor/edited; **trans.**, translated;
con., conductor; **dir.**, director;
f.sc., full score; **f.p.**, first performance;
mss., manuscript; **pub.**, publisher/published;
pos., posthumously; **inc.**, incomplete;
rev., revised/revision; **wd.**, withdrawn.

Section 1

Short titles

Music index
Opus numbers
A chronological conspectus

Prefatory note to the Index

The alphabetical arrangement of short titles which follows is cross-referenced and indexed to the full citations in **Part II, Section 2**. Brief notes are added parenthetically, where needed, as an aid to identification. The method of alphabetization ignores the definite and indefinite article. Likewise, any quantitative information in the title is disregarded in the alphabetical ordering, unless this is integral to the published or generally recognized title, e.g., "Two Pieces" would usually appear under "p," not "t," whereas "Sechs Hölderline-Fragmente" appears under "s," rather than "h." Occasionally a title is entered twice to facilitate research.

Music index

B

C

D

Dans les bois (orch.), 78
Dans les bois (v./pf.), 79
The Dark Tower (radio), 191
The Dark Valley (radio), 192
Death in Venice (opera), 227
Deus in adjutorium meum (v.), 282
Diaphenia (v./pf.), 94
Dido and Aeneas (realization), 396
Dinner Hour (film), 156
Diversions (pf./orch.), 348
Divertimento: Matinées musicales (orch.), 426
Divertimento: Soirées musicales (orch.), 425
Duchess of Malfi (theatre), 210
The Dynasts (radio), 193

E

The Eagle Has Two Heads (theatre), 211
Easter 1916 (theatre), 212
Eight Folk Songs (British Isles), 421
Einladung zur Martinsgans (v./pf.), 257
Elegy (str.), 80
Elegy (va.), 115
Elizabeth Variations (pf.), 95
Epitaph, The Clerk (v./pf.), 32
Etude (va.), 96
Four etudes symphoniques (pf.), 33
Evening Hymn (v.), 97
Everyone Sang (v./orch.), 116

F

G

H

M

N

O

Q

R

S

T

U

V

W

Y

Opus numbers

Britten gave opus numbers to ninety-five of his compositions. Numbers identified by an asterisk indicate that the composer reassigned that number to another composition. The letters [a] and [b] were assigned randomly.

1. *Sinfonietta*
2. *Phantasy*
3. *A Boy Was Born*
4. *Simple Symphony*
5. *Holiday Diary*
6. *Suite for Violin and Piano*
7. *Friday Afternoons*
8. *Our Hunting Fathers*
9. *Divertimento: Soirées musicales*
10. *Variations on a Theme of Frank Bridge*
11. *On This Island*
12. *Mont Juic*
13. *Piano Concerto*
14. *Ballad of Heroes*
15. *Violin Concerto*
16. *Young Apollo*
17* *Ad majorem Dei gloriam*
17. *Paul Bunyan*
18. *Les illuminations*
19. *Canadian Carnival*
20. *Sinfonia da requiem*
21. *Diversions*
22. *Seven Sonnets of Michelangelo*
23.1 *Introduction and Rondo alla Burlesca*
23.2 *Mazurka elegiaca*
24. *Divertimento: Matinées musicales*

25.   *String Quartet No. 1 in D*
26.   *Scottish Ballad*
27.* *An American Overture*
          (original title "Occasional Overture")
27.   *Hymn to St. Cecilia*
28.   *A Ceremony of Carols*
29.   *Prelude and Fugue*
30.   *Rejoice in the Lamb*
31.   *Serenade* (T/horn/st.)
32.   *Festival Te Deum*
33.   *Peter Grimes*
33a. *Peter Grimes: Four Sea Interludes*
33b. *Peter Grimes: Passacaglia*
34.   *The Young Person's Guide to the Orchestra*
35.   *The Holy Sonnets of John Donne*
36.   *String Quartet No. 2 in C*
37.   *The Rape of Lucretia*
38.   *Occasional Overture*
39.   *Albert Herring*
40.   *Canticle I: My Beloved is Mine*
41.   *A Charm of Lullabies*
42.   *Saint Nicolas*
43.   *The Beggar's Opera*
44.   *Spring Symphony*
45.   *The Little Sweep*
46.   *A Wedding Anthem* ("Amo ergo sum")
47.   *Five Flower Songs*
48.   *Lachrymae* (va./pf.)
48a. *Lachrymae* (va./str.)
49.   *Six Metamorphoses after Ovid*
50.   *Billy Budd*
51.   *Canticle II: Abraham and Isaac*
52.   *Winter Words*

A chronological conspectus

1932-1976

Music composed prior to 1932 may be found under Juvenilia.

1932

Ballet on a Basque Scenario
Concerto in B Minor for Viola, Violin, Orchestra
Phantasy (ob./vl./va./vc.)
Phantasy in F Minor (str. qt.)
Psalm 130: Out of the Deep (c./orch.)
Sinfonietta (chamber orch.)
Three Two-Part Songs:
    1. "The Ride-by-Nights," 2. "The Rainbow,"
    3. "The Ship of Rio."

1933

Alla quartetto serioso (str. qt.)
A Boy Was Born (v.)
Two Part-songs:
    1. "I Loved a Lass," 2. "Lift Boy."

1934

Holiday Diary (pf.)
Jubilate Deo in E Flat (c./org.)
May (v./pf.)
Simple Symphony (str. orch.)
Te Deum in C Major (c./org.)

1935

CTO (film))
Coal Face (film)
Conquering Space (film)
Dinner Hour (film)
Easter 1916 (theatre)
Friday Afternoons (v./pf.)
Gas/Coal Abstract (film)
God's Chillun (film)
GPO Title Music 1 & 2 (film)
How the Dial Works (film)
Two Insect Pieces (ob./pf.)
The King's Stamp (film)
Men Behind the Meters (film)
The New Operator (film)
A Poison Tree (v./pf.)
The Savings Bank (film)
Sorting Office (film)
Suite for Violin and Piano
Telegrams (film)
Timon of Athens (theatre)
Title Music III (film)
The Tocher (film)

1936

The Agamemnon of Aeschylus (theatre)
Around the Village Green (film)
Calendar of the Year (film)
Divertimento: Soirées musicales (orch.)
Four Barriers (film)
Line to the Tschierva Hut (film)
Love from a Stranger (feature film)
Lullaby for a Retired Colonel (pf.)

Men of the Alps (film)
Message from Geneva (film)
Mother Comfort (v./pf.)
Night Mail (film)
Our Hunting Fathers (v./orch)
Peace of Britain (film)
Phillip's Breeches (v.)
Russian Funeral (brass, perc.)
The Saving of Bill Blewitt (film)
Stay Down, Miner (theatre)
Temporal Variations (ob./pf.)
Theme (one of four improvised movements for organ)
Underneath the Abject Willow (v./pf.)
The Way to the Sea (film)

1937

The Ascent of F6 (theatre)
Book Bargain (film)
Cabaret Songs: Johnny, Funeral Blues, Jam Tart, (v./pf.)
The Company of Heaven (radio)
Fairest Isle (v./inst.)
Hadrian's Wall (radio)
King Arthur (radio)
Mont Juic (orch.)
Night Covers Up the Rigid Land (v./pf.)
On This Island (v./pf.)
Out of the Picture (theatre)
Pacifist March (v.)
Pagent of Empire (theatre)
Reveille (v./pf.)
The Sun Shines Down (v./pf.)
To Lie Flat on the Back (v./pf.)
Variations on a Theme of Frank Bridge (str. orch.)

1938

Advance Democracy (film)
Advance Democracy (motet)
Cabaret Songs: Tell Me the Truth About Love (v./pf.)
The Chartists' March (radio)
Cradle Song (v./pf.)
Fish in the Unruffled Lakes (v./pf.)
Lines on the Map (radio)
Mony a Pickle (film)
On the Frontier (theatre)
Piano Concerto
Spain (theatre)
They Walk Alone (theatre)
The World of the Spirit (radio)

1939

Ad majorem Dei gloriam (v.)
Ballad of Heroes (s./c./orch.)
Cabaret Songs: Calypso (v./pf.)
Canadian Carnival (orch.)
Johnson Over Jordan (theatre)
Les illuminations (v./pf.)
The Sword in the Stone (radio)
Violin Concerto
Young Apollo (pf./orch.)

1940

Dark Valley (radio)
Diversions (pf., left hand/orch.)
The Dynasts (radio)
Introduction and Rondo alla Burlesca (two pf.)
Les sylphides (orch.)

Seven Sonnets of Michelangelo (v./pf.)
Sinfonia da requiem (orch.)
Sonatina romantica (pf.)

1941

An American Overture (orch.)
Divertimento: Matinées musicales (orch.)
Mazurka elegiaca (two pf.)
Paul Bunyan (operetta)
The Rocking-Horse Winner (radio)
Scottish Ballad (two pf./orch.)
String Quartet No. 1

1942

American in England (radio series)
Appointment (radio)
Britain to America (radio series)
Ceremony of Carols (treble v./hp.)
Clarinet Concerto
God, Who Created Me (school anthem)
Hymn to St. Cecilia (c.)
If Thou Wilt Ease Thine Heart (v./pf.)
The Knotting Song (Purcell realization)
Lumberjacks of America (radio)
Man Born to Be King (radio)
O What is That Sound? (v./pf.)
Partita (chamber orch.)
Sleep, My Darling, Sleep (v./pf)
Village Organist's Piece
Voluntary ("Chorale Prelude in D Minor" for org.)
What the Wild Flowers Tell Me (Mahler arr., orch.)
What's on Your Mind? (v./pf.)
Who Is This in Garments Gory? (hymn arr.)
Wild with Passion (v./pf)

1943

Ballad of Little Musgrave and Lady Barnard (v./pf.)
Folk Songs, Vol. 1 (British Isles)
Four Freedoms No. 1: Pericles (radio)
Prelude and Fugue (str.)
Rejoice in the Lamb (s./c./org.)
The Rescue (radio)
Serenade (T/hn./str.)

1944

Festival Te Deum (c./org.)
A Poet's Christmas ("Chorale" for v.)
A Poet's Christmas ("A Shepherd's Carol" for v.)

1945

Deus in adjutorium meum (anthem)
The Golden Trio Sonata (Purcell arr., two v./vc./pf.)
Heigh-ho! Heigh-hi! (v.)
The Holy Sonnets of John Donne (v./pf.)
Peter Grimes (opera)
String Quartet No. 2 in C
This Way to the Tomb (theatre)

1946

The Dark Tower (radio)
Duchess of Malfi (theatre)
The Eagle Has Two Heads (theatre)
Folk Songs, Vol. 2 (France)
The Instruments of the Orchestra
Occasional Overture (orch.)
Prelude and Fugue on a Theme of Vittoria (org.)

The Queen's Epicedium (Purcell arr., v./pf.)
The Rape of Lucretia (opera)
The Young Person's Guide to the Orchestra

1947

Albert Herring (opera)
Canticle I: My Beloved Is Mine (v./pf.)
A Charm of Lullabies (v./pf.)
Folk Songs, Vol. 3 (British Isles)
Harmonia sacra (Purcell arr., v./pf.)
Men of Goodwill (radio)
Orpheus Britannicus: Seven Songs (Purcell arr., v./pf.)

1948

The Beggar's Opera
Orpheus Britannicus: Six Songs (Purcell arr., v./pf.)
Saint Nicolas (v./orch.)

1949

The Little Sweep ("Let's make an opera")
Spring Symphony (v./orch.)
Stratton (theatre)
Wedding Anthem, (S/T/c./org.)

1950

Five Flower Songs (c.)
Harmonia sacra: Job's Curse (Purcell arr., v./pf.)
Lachrymae (va./pf.)

1951

Billy Budd (opera)
Dido and Aeneas (Purcell realization)
Six Metamorphoses after Ovid (ob.)

1952

Canticle II: Abraham and Isaac (Alto/T/pf.)

1953

Gloriana (opera)
Variation on Sellinger's Round (orch.)
Winter Words (v./pf.)

1954

Am Stram Gram (theatre)
Canticle III: Still Falls the Rain (T/hn./pf.)
The Turn of the Screw (opera)

1955

Alpine Suite and Scherzo (recorders)
Farfield (1928-1930) (v./pf.)
Hymn to St. Peter (c./org.)
Punch Review ("Old Friends are Best") (theatre)
Timpani Piece for Jimmy (Blades)

1956

Antiphon
Orpheus Britannicus: Suite of Songs (Purcell arr., v./pf.)
The Prince of the Pagodas (ballet)
Prologue, Song and Epilogue (T/hn./pf.)

1957

Noye's Fludde (children's opera)
Songs from the Chinese (v./pf.)

1958

Einladung zur Martinsgans (v./pf.)
Nocturne (T/seven obbligato inst./str. orch.)
Sechs Hölderlin-Fragmente (v./pf.)

1959

Cantata academica (s./c./orch.)
Fanfare for St. Edmundsbury
Missa Brevis in D (boys' v./org.)

1960

Fanfare for S.S. Oriana
Folk Songs Vol. 4 (Ireland)
Harmonia sacra: Two Divine Hymns and Alleluia
A Midsummer Night's Dream (opera)
Orpheus Britannicus: Five Songs (Purcell arr., v./pf.)

1961

Cello Sonata in C
Fancie (v./pf.)
Folk Songs Vol. 5 (British Isles)
Folk Songs Vol. 6 (England)
Jubilate Deo (c./org.)
Orpheus Britannicus: Six Duets (Purcell arr., v./pf.)
Te Deum (c./org.)
Tom Bowling (v./pf.)

Venite exultemus Domino (c./org.)
War Requiem (S/T/baritone/c./boys' c./orch./org.)

1962

Hymn of St. Columba (c./org.)
Psalm 150 (children's v./inst.)
The Twelve Apostles (T/c./pf.)

1963

Cantata misericordium ((T/baritone/c./orch.)
Night Piece (pf.)
Nocturnal After John Dowland (guitar)
Symphony for Cello and Orchestra
The Ship of Rio (v./pf.)

1964

Cadenzas to Haydn's Cello Concerto in C
Cello Suite No. 1
Curlew River (church parable)

1965

Chacony in G Minor (Purcell arr., str.)
Gemini Variations (quartet for two players)
King Herod and the Cock (v./pf.)
Poet's Echo (v./pf.)
Songs and Proverbs of William Blake (baritone/pf.)
Voices for Today (c./org.)
When Night Her Purple Veil (Purcell arr. v./inst.)

1966

> *The Burning Fiery Furnace* (church parable)
> *Cadenzas to Mozart's Piano Concerto, No. 22*
> *Hankin Booby* (wind inst./perc.)

1967

> *The Building of the House* (orch.)
> *Cello Suite No. 2*
> *The Fairy Queen* (Purcell arr.)
> *The Oxen* (v./pf.)

1968

> *Children's Crusade* (v./orch.)
> *The Prodigal Son* (church parable)

1969

> *Five Spiritual Songs* (J.S. Bach arr., v./pf.)
> *Harp Suite in C*
> *Who Are These Children?* (T/pf.)

1970

> *Fanfare for D.W.*
> *Owen Wingrave* (opera for TV)

1971

> *Alleluia! Alec's 80th Birthday* (v.)
> *Canticle IV: Journey of the Magi* (three s.v./pf.)
> *Cello Suite No. 3*

1972-3

   Death in Venice (opera)

1974

   Canticle V: The Death of Saint Narcissus (T/hp.)
   Suite on English Folk Tunes (orch.)

1975

   A Birthday Hansel (v./hp.)
   Phaedra (v./small orch.)
   Sacred and Profane (v.)
   String Quartet No. 3

1976

   Christmas Cantata Sequence
   Eight Folk Songs, (British Isles)
   Lachrymae (va./str. orch.)
   Praise We Great Men (cantata)
   A Sea Symphony (orch.)
   Tema- 'Sacher' (vc.)
   Welcome Ode (young people's c./orch.)

Section 2

Full titles

Juvenilia
Incidental music
Stage music
Choral music
Solo vocal music
Instrumental music
Arrangements and editions

Note on Juvenilia

For purposes of convenience, the definition of 'juvenilia' adopted here is that of standard usage, i.e., the artistic fruits of childhood and youth. Inevitably, this limitation is challenged by such relatively 'mature' works of Britten's early creativity as the posthumously published *Quatre chansons françaises* (composed in the summer of 1928 at the age of 14 years and before Britten entered Gresham's School) and by a number of other musically significant works written during his youth. By his 18th birthday (22.xi.31), Britten had completed his first year of studies at the Royal College of Music and had already demonstrated a compositional facility and fertility which have been compared to that of Mozart in terms of their precocity and astonishing productivity. Neverthless, the demands of organization and orderly presentation of Britten's prodigious output during those early years of compositional activity require some use of conventions. To this end, the eighteenth birthday is deemed here to mark the closure of Britten's juvenilia period. Argument about the appropriateness of this arbitrary chronology can only serve to sharpen the reader's awareness and appreciation of Britten's early brilliance and evident genius.

Juvenilia

(<u>ca</u>. 1921-1931)

<u>ca</u>. 1921-1922

1. *Oh, That I'd Ne'er Been Married.*
   Robert Burns, v./pf., f.p. B-P Library, 20.v.76,
   pub. FM, 1985, as *Beware: Three Early Songs,*
   see citations II.5, II.30, note in published edition,
   BSB, p. 3.

2. *Symphony in C.*
   Orch., inc., *BSB,* p. 3.

3. *Symphony in F Major/Minor.*
   Vn./vc./pf., *BSB,* p. 3.

1923

4. *And Seeing the Multitudes,*
   Blessed Are They That Mourn.
   Recitative and aria, biblical text,
   v./pf., inc., *BSB,* p. 3.

5. *Beware.*
   Henry Wadsworth Longfellow, v./pf.,
   pub. FM, 1985, *Beware: Three Early Songs,*
   see citations II.1, II.30, *BSB,* p. 3.

6. *Felixtown.*
   Pf., inc., *BSB,* p. 5.

7. *Here We Go Up in a Flung Festoon.*
   Rudyard Kipling, v./pf., *BSB*, p. 3.

8. *Piece in A.*
   Vn./vc./db., *BSB*, p. 3.

9. *Piece in C.*
   Pf., inc., *BSB*, p. 3.

10. *Piece in D Flat.*
    Vn./pf., *BSB*, p. 3.

1924

11. *Allegro con spirito.*
    Pf., *BSB*, p. 5.

12. *Introduction.*
    Str., *BSB*, p. 5.

13. *Lento con introduczion* (*sic*)
    and allegro ma non troppo.
    Pf., inc., *BSB*, p. 5.

14. *Piece in C.*
    St. qt./pf., inc., *BSB*, p. 5.

15. *Piece in G.*
    Str., inc., *BSB*, p. 5.

1925

16. *Allegro.*
    Orch., inc., *BSB*, p. 5.

17. *Allegro molto e con brio.*
    Orch., inc., *BSB*, p. 5.

18. *Four Bourées.*
    Pf., *BSB*, p. 5.

19. *Seven Fantasias.*
    Pf., *BSB*, p. 5.

20. *Octett in D Major.*
    Str., *BSB*, p 5.

21. *Presto con molto fuoco.*
    Orch., *BSB*, p. 5.

22. *Six Scherzos.*
    Pf., *BSB* p. 5.

23. *Sonata in D.*
    Vn./pf., *BSB*, p. 5.

24. *Four Sonatas.*
    Pf., *BSB*, p. 5.

25. *Four Suites.*
    Pf., *BSB*, p. 5.

26. *Six Variations on*
    'How Bright These Glorious Spirits Shine,' by
    John Bacchus Dykes. C./str. qt./org./pf., *BSB*, p. 5.

27. *Ten Walztes* (*sic*).
    Pf., pub. FM, 1969, *Five Waltzes, BSB*, p. 5.

1926

28. *Adagio ma non troppo—allegro quasi presto;*
    Allegro.
    Orch., inc., *BSB*, p. 8.

29. *Allegro maestoso.*
    Pf./orch., inc., *BSB*, p. 8.

30. *The Brook.*
    V./vn., *BSB*, p. 7.

31. *Three Canons.*
    Va./pf., *BSB*, p. 7.

32. *Epitaph, The Clerk.*
    Herbert Asquith, v./pf., pub. FM, 1985,
    as *Beware: Three Early Songs,* see citations II.1, II.5.

33. *Four etudes symphoniques.*
    Pf., *BSB*, p. 5.

34. *Fantasia in A.*
    Pf., *BSB*, p. 7.

35. *First Loss.*
    Va./pf., *BSB*, p. 7.

36. *Mass in E Minor.*
    S./c./orch., *BSB*, p. 7.

37. *Mazurka in F Sharp Minor.*
    Pf., *BSB*, p. 7.

38. *Ouverture (sic)* ("Never Unprepared").
    Orch., *BSB*, p. 7.

39. *Overture No.1 in C.*
    Orch., *BSB*, p. 7.

40. *Piece in F Minor.*
    Inst. unspecified, inc., *BSB*, p. 8.

41. *Poème No. 1 in D.*
    Orch., *BSB*, p. 7.

42. *Poème No. 2 in B Minor.*
    Small orch., *BSB*, p. 9.

43. *Rondo capriccio.*
    Pf., *BSB*, p. 7 .

44. *Rondo in C Sharp Minor.*
    Pf., *BSB*, p. 7.

45. *Rondo in D.*
    Pf., *BSB*, p. 7.

46. *Sonata No. 8 in C Minor* ("Grand").
    Pf., *BSB*, p. 7.

47. *Sonata in A.*
    Vc./pf., *BSB*, p. 7.

48. *Sonata in C Minor.*
    Va./pf., *BSB*, p. 7.

49. *Sonata in F Sharp Minor*.
   Vn./va./vc., *BSB*, p. 7.

50. *Sonata in G Minor*.
   Vn./pf., *BSB*, p. 7.

51. *Sonata No. 9 in C Sharp Minor,* for piano.
   Pf., dedicated to Miss Ethel M.K. Astle,
   BSB, p. 7, *MRL*, p. 82.

52. *Sonate pour orgue ou pedale-pianoforte*.
   BSB, p. 7.

53. *Six Songs*.
   V./pf., dedicated to Mrs Edith Rhonda Britten,
   BSB, p. 9, *MRL,* p. 63.

54. *String Quartet in B Flat*.
   Inc., *BSB*, p. 8.

55. *String Quartet in G Minor*.
   BSB, p. 9.

56. *Suite fantastique in A Minor*.
   Orch. with piano obbligato. *BSB*, p. 7.

57. *Suite No. 5 in F*.
   Pf., *BSB*, p. 5.

58. *Three Toccatas*.
   Pf., *BSB*, p. 5.

59. *Trio in Fantastic Form in C*.
   Vn./va./pf., *BSB*, p. 7.

60. *Trio in Fantastic Form in E Minor.*
    Vn./va./pf.,. *BSB*, p. 7.

1927

61. *Cavatina in A.*
    Str. qt., *BSB*, p. 9.

62. *Chaos and Cosmos: Symphonic Poem in E.*
    Orch., *BSB*, p. 9.

63. *Kyrie* and *Requiem in B Minor.*
    C./orch., *BSB*, p. 9.

64. *Four Nursery Rhymes.*
    Anon., v./pf., *BSB*, p. 9.

65. *Poème No. 3 in E.*
    Small orch., *BSB*, p. 9.

66. *Poème No. 4 in B Flat.*
    Small orch., *BSB*, p. 9.

67. *Poème No. 5 in F Sharp Minor.*
    Small orch., *BSB*, p. 9.

68. *Three Poems.*
    Str. qt., *BSB*, p. 11.

69. *Prometheus Unbound.* (B flat).
    Percy Bysshe Shelley, (fragment), c./str./pf., *BSB*, p. 9.

70. *Rhapsodie.*
    pf., *BSB*, p. 11.

71. *Eight Sacred Rounds.*
     V., *BSB*, p. 9.

72. *Sonata No. 10 in B Flat.*
     Pf., *BSB*, p. 11.

73. *Sonatina.*
     Va./pf., *BSB*, p. 11.

74. *String Quartet in A Minor.*
     BSB, p. 9.

75. *String Quartet in G.*
     BSB, p. 9.

76. *Symphony in D Minor.*
     Orch., *BSB*, p. 9.

1928

77. *Allegro moderato, Presto.*
     Orch., two versions, inc., *BSB*, p. 12.

78. *Dans les bois.*
     Orch., *BSB*, p. 11.

79. *Dans les bois.*
     Gérard de Nerval, S/pf., *BSB*, p. 11.

80. *Elegy.*
     Str., *BSB*, p. 11.

81. *Humoreske (sic) in C.*
Orch., *BSB*, p. 11.

82. *Menuetto.*
Pf., *BSB*, p. 11.

83. *Novelette.*
Str. qt., *BSB*, p. 13.

84. *Of a' the Airts.*
Robert Burns, v./pf., *BSB*, p. 13.

85. *Piece.*
Pf., *BSB*, p. 11.

86. *Quatre chansons françaises.*
Song-cycle, v./orch., f.p. London, BBC, 30.iii.80,
"Chanson d'automme," Verlaine,
"L'enfrance," Hugo,
"Nuits de juin," Hugo,
"Sagesse," Verlaine,
"Mon rêve familier," Verlaine, discarded,
v./pf.version pub. FM, 1982, full score pub. 1983,
BSB, pp. 12, 13, 30.

87. *Sonata No. 11 in B.*
Pf., *BSB*, p. 11.

88. *Sonatina.*
Pf., *BSB*, p. 13.

89. *String Quartet in F.*
BSB, p. 11.

90. *Tit for Tat: Silver.*
    Walter de la Mare, v./pf., f.p. 23.vi.69, AF,
    rev. 1968, pub. FM, 1969, as *Tit for Tat,*
    see citations II.108, II.146, *BSB*, p. 11.

91. *Trio in G Minor.*
    Vn./va./pf., *BSB*, p. 11.

92. *The Waning Moon.*
    Percy Bysshe Shelley, v./pf., *BSB*, p. 11.

1929

93. *Children of Love.*
    Hector Henry Munro ('Saki'), women's v., *BSB*, p. *15.*

94. *Diaphenia.*
    Henry Constable, T/pf., *BSB*, p. 15.

95. *Elizabeth Variations.*
    Pf., *BSB*, p. 13.

96. *Etude.*
    Va., *BSB*, p. 15.

97. *Evening Hymn.*
    SATB c., rev. from 1923, *BSB*, p. 15.

98. *Introduction and allegro.*
    Va./str., *BSB*, p. 15.

99. *Lilian.*
    Alfred, Lord Tennyson, v./pf., *BSB*, p. 15.

100. *Miniature Suite*.
    Str. qt., *BSB*, p. 215.

101. O*h Why Did E'er My Thoughts Aspire*.
    Charles Sackville, v./pf., *BSB*, p. 13.

102. *The Owl*.
    Alfred, Lord Tennyson, v./pf., *BSB*, p. 15.

103. *Two Pieces*.
    Vn./va./pf., *BSB*, p. 15.

104. *The Quartette*.
    Walter de la Mare, v. qt., *BSB*, p. 13.

105. *Rhapsody*.
    Str. qt., *BSB*, p. 13.

106. *Rhapsody*.
    Vn./va./pf., *BSB*, p. 15.

107. *Two Songs*.
    John Fletcher, mixed v. qt., *BSB*, p. 15.

108. *A Song of Enchantment, Tit for Tat*.
    Walter de la Mare, v./pf., rev. 1968, pub. FM, 1969,
    Tit for Tat, see citations II.90, II.146, *BSB*, pp. 13, 23.

109. *Wild Time*.
    Walter de la Mare, S/str., *BSB*, p. 15.

110. *Witches Song*.
    Ben Jonson, v./pf., *BSB*, p. 15.

1930

111. *Ah Fly Not, Pleasure, Pleasant-Hearted Pleasure.*
        V./pf., W.S. Blunt, *BSB*, p. 17.

112. *Bagatelle.*
        Vn./va./pf., *BSB*, p. 15.

113. *The Birds.*
        Hilaire Belloc, v./str., RCM scholarship,
        rev. 1934, pub. BH, *BSB*, p. 17.

114. *Chamber Music (V).*
        James Joyce, S or T/pf., *BSB*, p. 17.

115. *Elegy.*
        Va., pub. FM, 1985, *BSB*, p. 17.

116. *Everyone Sang.*
        Siegfried Sassoon, T/small orch., *BSB*, p. 15.

117. *A Hymn to the Virgin.*
        Anthem, mixed v., rev.1934, pub. BH, *BSB*, p. 17.

118. *I Saw Three Witches.*
        Walter de la Mare, S/A/pf., *BSB*, p. 19.

119. *A Little Idyll.*
        Pf., *BSB*, p. 15.

120. *May in the Greenwood.*
        V./pf., *BSB*, p. 17.

121. *Nurse's Song.*
      William Blake, S/A/pf., *BSB*, p. 17.

122. *Piece.*
      Va./pf., *BSB*, p. 17.

123. *Three Character Pieces.*
      'For John Boyd, Daphne Black, and Michael Tyler.'
      Pf., f.p. Chester Town Hall, 28.vii.89, pub. FM, 1989,
      BSB, p. 17, *KBR*, p. 306

124. *A Poem of Hate.*
      Pf., *BSB*, p. 15.

125. *Quartettino.*
      Str. qt., pub. FM, 1984, *BSB*, p. 15.

126. *Sextet,* for flute. oboe, clarinet, bass clarinet, horn,
      Fl./ob./cl./bcl./hn./bn., *BSB*, p. 17.

127. *Sketch No. 1.*
      'For D. Layton.' Str., *BSB*, p. 17.

128. *Sketch No. 2.*
      'For E.B.B.' Va./str., *BSB*, p. 17.

129. *The Sycamore Tree* ("I Saw Three Ships").
      Carol for SATB, f.p. Lowestoft, St. John's, 5.i.31,
      rev. 1967, pub. FM, *BSB*, p. 47.

130. *To Electra: I Dare Not Ask a Kisse.*
      Robert Herrick, v./pf., *BSB*, p. 17.

131. *Wealden Trio: The Song of the Women.*
     Ford Madox Ford, carol for un. women's voices,
     f.p. AF, 9.vi.68, rev. pub. FM, 1967, *BSB*, p. 17.

132. *A Widow Bird Sate Mourning For Her Love.*
     Percy Bysshe Shelley, v./pf., *BSB*, p. 19.

1931

133. *Three Fugues.*
     Pf., *BSB*, p. 21.

134. *Love Me Not for Comely Grace.*
     Text anon., madrigal, SSAT,
     BSB, p. 19, *MKL*, p. 156.

135. *Mass.*
     Four v., *BSB*, p. 19.

136. *The Moth.*
     Walter de la Mare, baritone/pf., *BSB*, p. 19.

137. *O Lord, Forsake Me Not.*
     Text from Psalms 28, 38, 39, 116,
     motet for double chorus,
     BSB, p. 19, *MRL*, p. 159.

138. *Two Pieces.*
     "The Moon" (after Percy Bysshe Shelley),
     "Going Down Hill on a Bicycle"
             (after Henry Charles Beeching).
     Vn./pf., *BSB*, p. 21.

139. *Plymouth Town.*
    Ballet score, (after Violet Alford),
    small orch., inc., *BSB*, p. 21.

140. *Psalm 150: Praise Ye the Lord.*
    Mendelssohn Scholarship entry, c./orch.,
    see citation II.246, "Two Psalms," *BSB*, pp. 20-21.

141. *Three Small Songs.*
    S/orch., f.p. Snape, 6.x.86,
      "Aspatia's Song," John Fletcher,
      "Hymn to Pan," John Fletcher,
      "Love Is a Sickness," Samuel Daniel,
    BSB, p. 21, *MRL*, p. 186.

142. *Sport.*
    W.H. Davies, B/pf., *BSB*, p. 19.

143. *String Quartet in D Major.*
    F.p. AF, 7.vi.75, rev. pub. FM, 1974,
    BSB, p. 21.

144. *Sweet Was the Song the Virgin Sung.*
    Robert Southwell, carol for women's v.,
    f.p. AF, 15.vi.68, rev.1966, pub. FM,
    "Thy King's Birthday,"
    see citation II.145, *BSB*, p. 19, *KBR*, p. 297.

145. *Thy King's Birthday.*
    Robert Southwell and the Bible, S/A/chorus,
    "Christmas Suite; New Prince, New Pomp,"
    f.p. AF, 24.vi.55, see citation II.144,
    BSB 19, 81, *KBR*, p. 297

146. *Tit for Tat: Autumn,* and *Vigil.*
Walter de la Mare, B or A/pf.,
"Autumn" originally for v./str. qt.,
f.p. AF, 23.vi.69, rev. 1968,
pub. FM, 1969, as *Tit for Tat,*
see citations II.90, II.108, *BSB*, p. 19.

147. *To the Willow-tree.*
Robert Herrick, madrigal, SATB,
BSB, p. 19, *MRL*, p. 158.

148. *Twelve Variations on a Theme.*
Pf., pub. FM, 1986,
BSB, p. 21.

Incidental music

Film
Radio
Theatre

Detailed information on Britten's incidental music is found in a *Catalogue raisonné* compiled by John Evans and Philip Reed (*A Britten Source Book* [Evans/Reed/Wilson, 1987]). Philip Reed's PhD dissertation (East Anglia, 1987) may be consulted for additional particulars regarding sources and performance information. Acknowledgment and location of the information included here is provided as the last item of each citation.

Film

149. *Advance Democracy.*
      Realistic Film Unit, 1938, c./perc.,
      different music from motet of same name, *BSB*, p. 143.

150. *Around the Village Green.*
      Travel & Industrial Development Assoc., 1936,
      fl./ob./cl./trpt./trbn./timp./hp./str., *BSB*, p. 139.

151. *Book Bargain.*
      GPO, 1937, pf./pic./cl./perc., *BSB*, p. 142.

152. *Calendar of the Year.*
      GPO, 1936, WHA,
      fl./cl./trpt./trbn./hp./str. qnt./perc., *BSB*, p. 139.

153. *Coal Face.*
     GPO, 1935, WHA, Montague Slater,
     v./whistler/c./pf./perc., *BSB*, p. 132.

154. *Conquering Space* ("Modern Communications").
     GPO, 1935, pf./fl./ob./cl./bn./perc., *BSB*, p. 136.

155. *CTO* ("The Story of the Central Telegraph Office").
     GPO, 1935, pf./fl./ob./cl./perc., *BSB*, p. 134.

156. *Dinner Hour.*
     British Commercial Gas Association, 1935,
     pf./fl./cl./vn./vc./perc., *BSB*, p. 135.

157. *Four Barriers.*
     GPO, 1936, mss. missing, *BSB*, p. 141.

158. *Gas Abstract* ("Coal Abstract").
     British Commercial Gas Assoc., 1935,
     pf./fl./cl./bn./perc., *BSB*, p. 134

159. *God's Chillun* ("Negroes").
     GPO, STB/c./pf./ob./hp./perc.,
     BSB, p. 134.

160. *How the Dial Works.*
     GPO, 1935, pf./fl./ob./cl./perc., *BSB*, p. 136.

161. *The Instruments of the Orchestra.*
     Crown Film Unit, see citation II.342, *The Young
     Person's Guide to The Orchestra,* Op. 34, *BSB*, p. 143.

162. *The King's Stamp.*
     GPO, 1935, pf./fl./cl./perc., George V Jubilee,
     BB's first GPO commission, *BSB*, pp. 29, 131.

163. *Line to the Tschierva Hut* ("Swiss Telephone").
     GPO, 1936, fl./cl./trpt./hp./str. qnt./perc.,
     (Swiss Alpine Hut at Pontresina), *BSB*, p. 140.

164. *Love from a Stranger.*
     Trafalgar Films (BB's only feature film), 1936,
     fl./ob./cl./sax./bn./trpt./trbn./hp./str./perc.,
     f.p. 7.i.37, *BSB*, p. 141.

165. *Men Behind the Meters.*
     British Commercial Gas Assoc., 1935,
     pf./fl./ob./cl./vn./vc./perc., *BSB*, p. 135.

166. *Men of the Alps.*
     GPO, 1936, fl./cl./trpt./hp./str./perc.,
     includes music by Rossini, *BSB*, p. 140.

167. *Message from Geneva.*
     GPO, 1936, *BSB*, p. 140.

168. *Mony a Pickle.*
     GPO, 1938, pf./fl./cl./perc., *BSB*, p. 143.

169. *The New Operator.*
     GPO, 1935, pf./fl./ob./cl./bn./perc., *BSB*, p. 137.

170. *Night Mail* and *GPO Title Music 1 and 2.*
     GPO, 1936, WHA, fl./ob./bn./trpt./hp./str. qt./perc.,
     BSB, pp. 138, 139.

171. *Peace of Britain.*
     Strand Films, pf./fl./cl./trpt./str./perc.,
     BSB, p. 139.

172. *The Saving of Bill Blewitt.*
     GPO, 1936, fl./cl./trpt./trbn./hp./str./perc.,
     mss. missing, *BSB*, p. 141.

173. *The Savings Bank.*
     GPO, 1935, pf./fl./ob./cl./bn./perc., GPO, 1935,
     BSB, p. 137.

174. *Sorting Office.*
     GPO, 1935, pf./fl./ob./cl./bn./perc., *BSB*, p. 137.

175. *Telegrams.*
     GPO (attribution problematic), 1935,
     v./pf./fl./ob./cl./perc., GPO, 1935, *BSB*, p. 133.

176. *Title Music III.*
     British Commercial Gas Assoc., 1935,
     pf./fl./cl./vn./vc./perc., *BSB*, p. 136.

177. *The Tocher.*
     GPO, 1935, Rossini, arr. BB, v./inst.,
     silhouette film, Reiniger animator, *BSB*, p. 133.

178. *The Way to the Sea.*
     Strand Films for Southern Railways, 1936,
     WHA, commentator/inst., *BSB*, p. 142.

Radio

179. *American in England: The Anglo-American Angle.*
    BBC/CBS, 7.ix.42, orch.,
    Royal Air Force Orch., *BSB*, p. 161.

180. *American in England: London by Clipper.*
    BBC/CBS, 27.vii.42, pf./orch.,
    Royal Air Force Orch., *BSB*, p. 159.

181. *American in England: London to Dover.*
    BBC/CBS, 10.viii.42, orch.,
    Royal Air Force Orch., *BSB*, p. 159.

182. *American in England: Ration Island.*
    BBC/CBS, 17.viii.42, pf./orch.,
    Royal Air Force Orch., *BSB*, p. 160.

183. *American in England: Women of Britain.*
    BBC/CBS, 24.viii.42, orch.,
    Royal Air Force Orch., *BSB*, p. 161.

184. *American in England: The Yanks Are Here.*
    BBC/CBS, 31.viii.42, pf./orch.,
    Royal Air Force Orch., *BSB*, p. 161.

185. *Appointment.*
    BBC, 22.vii.42, Norman Corwin,
    orch., *BSB*, p. 159.

186. *Britain to America: Britain through American Eyes,* 1-9.
    BBC/NBC, 20.ix.42, Louis MacNeice,
    orch., LSO, *BSB*, p. 162.

187. *Britain to America: Where Do I Come In?* II-4.
        BBC/NBC, 7.x.42, Louis MacNeice,
        orch. LSO, *BSB*, p. 162.

188. *Britain to America: Where Do We Go From Here?* II-13.
        BBC/NBC, 3.i.43, Louis MacNeice,
        orch., LSO, *BSB*, p. 162.

189. *The Chartists' March.*
        BBC, 13.v.38, c./perc.,
        BSB, p. 156.

190. *The Company of Heaven.*
        BBC, 29.ix.37, BB's first collaboration with PP,
        S/T/c./timp./org./str.,
        see citation II.245, *BSB*, p. 154.

191. *The Dark Tower.*
        BBC, 21.i.46, Louis MacNeice, trpt./str./perc.,
        BSB, p. 164.

192. *The Dark Valley.*
        CBS, 2.vi.40, WHA,
        v./fl./ca./cl./trpt./perc., *BSB*, p. 158.

193. *The Dynasts.*
        CBS, 1940, Thomas Hardy, brass/str./perc.,
        BSB, p. 158.

194. *Four Freedoms No. 1: Pericles.*
        BBC, 21.ii.43, Louis MacNeice,
        mss. missing, scoring unknown, *BSB*, p.163.

195. *Hadrian's Wall.*
    BBC, 25.x.37, WHA, v./str. qt./perc.,
    see citation II.397, mss. missing, *BSB*, p. 155.

196. *King Arthur.*
    BBC, 23.iv.37, D. Geoffrey Bridson, v./orch.,
    LSO, *BSB*, p. 154.

197. *Lines on the Map.*
    BBC, 1938, trpt./trbn./perc., *BSB*, p. 155.

198. *Lumberjacks of America* ("Timber").
    BBC, 24.viii.42, Ranald MacDougall,
    survey of US timber industry, orch., *BSB*, p. 160.

199. *The Man Born to be King No. 10,* "The Princes of this World." BBC, 23.viii.42, v./pf., BS*B*, p. 160.

200. *The Man born to be King No. 11*, "The King of Sorrows." BBC, 20.ix.42, v./pf., *BSB*, p. 162.

201. *Men of Goodwill: The Reunion of Christmas.*
    BBC, 25.xii.47, Lawrence Gilliam, Leonard Cottrell, orch., LSO, pub. 1982, *Men of Goodwill: Orchestral Variations, BSB*, p. 165.

202. *A Poet's Christmas* (two choral settings by Britten).
    BBC, 24.xii.44, WHA, SSAATTBB,
      "Chorale," after an old French carol,
      "A Shepherd's Carol" ('O Lift Your Little Pinkie'),
    second item pub. Novello, 1962, *BSB*, p. 164.

203. *The Rescue.*
>   BBC, 4.xii.43, Sackville-West, v./pf./orch.,
>   *BSB*, p. 163.

204. *The Rocking-Horse Winner.*
>   CBS, 6.iv.41, WHA, James Stern, D.H. Lawrence,
>   v./inst. (mss. missing), *BSB*, p. 158.

205. *The Sword in the Stone.*
>   BBC, six programmes serialized 11.v.-16.vii.39,
>   Marianne Helweg adapted from novel by T.H. White,
>   v./ins. *BSB*, pp. 41, 157.

206. *World of the Spirit.*
>   BBC, 5.v.38, R. Ellis Roberts, comp., v./orch.,
>   *BSB* p. 156.

Theatre

207. *The Agamemnon of Aeschylus.*
>   London, Group Theatre, Westminster Theatre, 9.x.36,
>   SATB/fl./ca./cl./perc., *BSB*, p. 33, *BRI*, p. 288.

208. *Am Stram Gram.*
>   London, Toynbee Hall Theatre, 4.iii.54,
>   André Roussin, v./pf., *BSB*, pp. 79, 153.

209. *The Ascent of F6.*
>   London, Group-Mercury Theatre, 26.ii.37,
>   WHA. Christopher Isherwood, v./inst.,
>   see citation II.292, "Cabaret Songs,"
>   *BSB*, pp. 35, 146.

210. *Duchess of Malfi.*
New York, Barrymore Theater, 1946,
John Webster, adapted by WHA,
mss. missing, *BSB*, pp. 63, 152.

211. *The Eagle Has Two Heads.*
London, Hammersmith-Lyric Theatre, 1946,
Jean Cocteau, trans. by Ronald Duncan,
brass/perc., *BSB*, pp. 63, 151, 152.

212. *Easter 1916.*
London, Islington Town Hall, Left Theatre, 4.xii.35,
Montagu Slater, v./acc./perc.,
mss. missing, *BSB* 31, 145.

213. *Johnson Over Jordan.*
London, New Theatre, 22.ii.39,
J.B. Priestley, orch., *BSB*, pp. 41, 150.

214. *On the Frontier.*
Cambridge, Cambridge Arts Theatre, 14.i.38,
WHA, Christopher Isherwood, pf./acc./trpt./perc./v.,
BSB, pp. 39, 149.

215. *Out of the Picture.*
London, Westminster Theatre, 5.xii.37,
Louis MacNeice, orch., *BSB*, pp. 37, 148.

216. *Pageant of Empire.*
London, Collins' Music Hall, 28.ii.37,
Montagu Slater, orch., *BSB*, pp. 35, 147.

217. *Punch Review.*
     London, Duke of York's Theatre, 8.ix.55,
     WHA, William Plomer, v./pf., "Old Friends Are Best,"
     "Tell Me the Truth about Love,"
     BSB, pp 81, 153.

218. *Spain.*
     London, Mercury Theatre, Puppet Show, 1938,
     Montagu Slater, v./cl./vn./pf.,
     (mss. missing), *BSB*, pp. 39, 148.

219. *Stay Down, Miner.*
     London. Westminster Theatre, 10.iv.36,
     Montagu Slater, v./cl./perc./vn./vc., *BSB*, pp. 31, 145.

220. *Stratton.*
     Brighton, Theatre Royal, EOG, 31.x.49,
     Ronald Duncan, (mss. missing), *BSB*, pp. 71, 152.

221. *They Walk Alone.*
     London, "Q" Theatre, 21.xi.38, Max Catto, org.,
     BB's first commercial theatre, *BSB*, pp. 41, 150.

222. *This Way to the Tomb.*
     London, Mercury Theatre, 11.x.45,
     Ronald Duncan, v./perc./pf., see citation II.282,
     "Deus in adjutorium meum," 3 songs from
     "This Way to the Tomb," pub. FM, 1988,
     v./hp./pf., B*SB*, pp. 61, 151.

223. *Timon of Athens.*
     London, Westminster Theatre, 19.xi.35,
     William Shakespeare, ob./harpsichord/perc.,
     BSB, pp. 29, 144.

Stage music

Ballet
Opera
Church parables

Ballet

224. *The Prince of the Pagodas,* Op. 57.
    John Cranko, choreographer, 3 act, 1956,
    f.p. London, ROH-CG, Royal Ballet, 1.i.57,
    pub. BH, *BSB*, p. 83.

Opera

225. *Albert Herring,* Op. 39.
    Guy de Maupassant, ad. Eric Crozier, 1947, 3 act,
    f.p. Sussex: GOH, EOG, 20.vi.47,
    pub. BH, *BSB*, pp. 64, 65, *BRI*, p. 287.

226. *Billy Budd,* Op. 50.
    Herman Melville, ad. Eric Crozier, E.M. Forster, 1951,
    4 act, 1960, rev. 2 act, f.p. London, ROH-CG, 1.xii.51
    pub. BH, *BSB*, pp. 75, 90.

227. *Death in Venice,* Op. 88.
    Thomas Mann, ad. Myfanwy Piper, 1973, 2 act,
    f.p. AF, ECO, EOG, 16.vi.73,
    pub. FM, *BSB*, pp. 119, 121, *KBR*, p. 288.

228. *Gloriana,* Op. 53.
     William Plomer, 1953, 2 act, rev. 1966,
     f.p. London, ROH-CG, 8.vi.53,
     pub. BH, *BSB*, p. 77.

229. *The Little Sweep* ("Let's Make an Opera"), Op. 45.
     Eric Crozier, 1949, children's opera,
     f.p. AF, EOG, 14.vi.49, pub. BH, *BSB*, p. 71.

230. *A Midsummer Night's Dream,* Op. 64.
     William Shakespeare, 1960, 3 act, ad. BB, PP,
     f.p. AF, EOG, 11.vi.60, pub. BH, *BSB*, p. 91.

231. *Noye's Fludde,* Op. 59.
     Chester Miracle Play, set for adults', children's v.,
     chamber ensemble, children's orch., 1957,
     f.p. AF, Orford Parish Church, 18.vi.58,
     pub. BH, *BSB,* p. 85, *BRI,* p. 288.

232. *Owen Wingrave,* Op. 58.
     Henry James, ad. Myfanwy Piper, 1970, 2 acts, for TV,
     f.p. BBC TV, EOG, ECO, 16.v.71,
     pub. FM, *BSB*, p. 115, *BRI,* p. 288.

233. *Paul Bunyan,* Op. 17.
     W.H. Auden, 1941, wd., rev. 1974, operetta,
     f.p. New York, 5.v.41,
     pub. FM, 1974, *BSB*, pp. 45, 47.

234. *Peter Grimes,* Op. 33.
     Montagu Slater, 1945, 3 act,
     f.p. London, Sadler's Wells, 7.vi.45,
     pub. BH, *BSB*, p. 57.

235. *The Rape of Lucretia,* Op. 37.
      Ronald Duncan, 1946, rev. 1947, 2 act,
      f.p. Sussex, Glyndebourne Opera Festival, 12.vii.46,
      pub. BH, *BSB*, p. 61, *BRI*, p. 287.

236. *Turn of the Screw,* Op. 54.
      Henry James, ad. Myfanwy Piper, 1954, 2 act,
      f.p. Venice, Teatro La Fenice, 7.ix.54,
      pub. BH, *BSB*, p. 79, *BRI*, p. 28.

Church parables

237. *The Burning Fiery Furnace,* Op. 77.
      William Plomer, 1966,
      f.p. AF, Orford Parish Church, EOG, 9.vi.66,
      pub. FM, *BSB*, pp. 105, 106.

238. *Curlew River,* Op. 71.
      William Plomer, 1964,
      f.p. AF, Orford Parish Church, EOG, 12.vi.64,
      pub. FM, *BSB*, p. 99, *BRI*, p. 288.

239. *The Prodigal Son,* Op. 81.
      William Plomer, 1968,
      f.p. AF, Orford Parish Church, 10.vi.68,
      pub. FM, *BSB*, p. 109, *BRI*, p. 288.

NB. *The Beggar's Opera,* Op. 43.
See citation II.424, under Arrangements and editions.

Choral music

Voices with orchestra
Voices with keyboard or harp
Unison choral music
A cappella choral music
Unfinished choral works

Voices with orchestra

240. *Ballad of Heroes,* Op. 14.
W.H. Auden, Randall Swingler, cantata,
T or S s./c./orch., f.p. London, Queen's Hall, 5.iv.39,
pub. BH, *BSB*, p. 41, *BRI*, p. 295.

241. *Building of the House,* Op. 79.
Psalm 127, orch., (c. optional), 1967,
f.p. AF, ECO, 2.vi.67, pub. FM, see citation II.332,
BSB, pp. 106, 107.

242. *Cantata academica* ("Carmen basiliense"), Op. 62.
Latin texts, Bernhard Wyss, comp., SATB s./c./orch.,
1959, f.p. Switzerland, Basle University, 1.vi.60,
pub. BH, *BSB*, p. 89.

243. *Cantata misericordium,* Op. 69.
T/baritone, s./small c./str./pf./hp./perc.,
Latin text, Patrick Wilkinson, f.p. Geneva, 1.ix.63,
pub. BH, *BSB*, p. 97.

244. *Children's Crusade* ("Kinderkreuzzug"), Op. 82.
Bertolt Brecht, ballad for children's c./orch., 1968,
f.p. London, St. Paul's Cathedral, 19.v.69,
pub. FM, *BSB*, pp. 109, 111, *BRI*, p 296.

245. *The Company of Heaven.*
Concert version. Texts selected by R. Ellis Roberts,
speaker/v./timp./str./org.,
f. concert p. AF, 10.vi.89, pub. FM,
see citation II.190, *BSB*, pp. 37, 154, 155.

246. *Two Psalms.*
V./orch., 1932,
    "Out of the Deep," Psalm 130,
    "Praise Ye the Lord," Psalm 150,
see citation II.140, *BSB*, pp. 20, 21.

247. *Psalm 150,* Op. 67.
Children's v./inst., 1962, f.p. AF, 24.vi.63,
pub. BH, *BSB*, pp. 95, 97.

248. *Saint Nicolas,* Op. 42.
Eric Crozier, cantata for T s./SATB/boys' v./str. orch.,
pf./perc./org., f.p. AF, 5.vi.48, BH, *BSB*, p. 69.

249. *Spring Symphony,* Op. 44.
S/A/T, s./c./orch., texts by WHA, Barnefield,
Blake, Beaument/Fletcher, Clare, Herrick, Milton,
Nashe, Peel, Spenser, Vaughan,
f.p. Amsterdam, 9.vii.49,
pub. BH, *BSB*, p. 71, *BRI*, p. 295.

250. *Variations on a French Carol.*
   Carol of the Deanery of Saint-Ménéhould,
   Women's voices, pf./vn./va., f.p. 1.xii.31, *BSB*, p. 21.

251. *War Requiem,* Op. 66.
   The missa pro defunctis and poems by Wilfred Owen,
   S/T/B s./m.f.c./boys' c./two orch./org./piano, 1961,
   f.p. Coventry, St. Michael's Cathedral., 30.v.62,
   pub. BH, *BSB*, p. 95, *BRI*, p. 295.

252. *Welcome Ode,* Op. 95.
   17th/18th cent. English lyrics, anon., Thomas Dekker,
   Henry Fielding, Ford Madox Ford, c./SAB/orch.,
   1976, f.p. Ipswich, 11.vii.77, pub. FM, *BSB*, p. 125.

Voices with keyboard or harp

253. *Antiphon,* Op. 56b.
   George Herbert, c./org., f.p. Tenbury Wells, 29.ix.56,
   pub. BH, *BSB*, p. 83.

254. *Ballad of Little Musgrave and Lady Barnard.*
   Text anon., v./pf., 1943, f.p. February 1944,
   Germany, Eichstatt POW Camp., pub. BH, *BSB*. p. 57.

255. *A Boy Was Born,* Op. 3.
   Choral variations, anon., Francis Quarles, Christina
   Rosetti, Thomas Tusser, men's, women's, boys' v.,
   org. (ad lib.), 1933, f.p. BBC, 23.ii.34, rev. 1955,
   pub. OUP, *BSB*, pp. 22, 25.

256. *A Ceremony of Carols,* Op. 28.
   Treble v./hp. or pf., f.p. Norwich Castle, 5.xii.42,
   rev. 1943, pub. BH, *BSB*, pp. 51, 53, *BRI*, pp 298-9.

257. *Einladung zur Martinsgans.*
　　　V./pf., 1958, Hurlimann 60th birthday, *BSB*, p. 87.

258. *God, Who Created Me.*
　　　Henry Charles Beeching, school anthem, c./org., 1942,
　　　BSB, p. 49.

259. *The Golden Vanity,* Op. 78.
　　　Colin Graham, English ballad adaptation, a vaudeville
　　　for boys v./pf., 1966, f.p. AF, 3.vi.67, pub. FM,
　　　BSB, p. 105.

260. *A Hymn of St. Columba* ("Regis regum rectissimi").
　　　C./org., 1962, N. Ireland, Ulster Singers, 2.vi.63,
　　　pub. BH, *BSB*, p. 97.

261. *Hymn to St. Peter,* Op. 56a.
　　　Gradual for the Feast of St. Peter and St. Paul, c./org.,
　　　1955, f.p. Norwich, St. Peter's Choir, 20.xi.55,
　　　pub. BH, *BSB* 81

262. *Jubilate Deo in E Flat.*
　　　C./org., 1934, pub. FM, 1984, *BSB*, p. 27.

263. *Jubilate Deo.*
　　　C./org., 1961, f.p. Leeds Parish Church, 8.x.61,
　　　pub. OUP, *BSB*, pp. 93, 95.

264. *Missa brevis in D,* Op. 63.
　　　Boys' v./org., 1959, BH, *BSB*, p. 89.

265. *The Oxen* ("Christmas Eve, and Twelve of the Clock").
　　　Thomas Hardy, carol for two-part women's c./pf.,
　　　1967, pub. FM, *BSB*, p. 107.

266. *Festival Te Deum,* Op. 32.
    C./org., 1944, f.p. Swindon, St. Mark's, 24.iv.45,
    pub. BH, *BSB*, p. 57.

267. *Rejoice in the Lamb* ("Jubilate agno"), Op. 30.
    Christopher Smart, festival cantata,
    treble, alto, T/B, s., SATB c./org.,
    f.p. Northampton, St. Matthew's Church, 21.ix.43,
    pub. BH, *BSB*, p. 55.

268. *Te Deum in C Major.*
    C./org., St. Michael's Singers, Cornhill, 13.xi.35,
    pub. OUP, *BSB*, pp. 27, 29.

269. *Three Two-part Songs.*
    Walter de la Mare, boys' or women's v./pf.,
    f.p. London, Mercury Theatre, 12.xii.32,
        "The Ride-by-Nights," "The Rainbow,"
        "The Ship of Rio,"
    see citation II.324 for arr. of "The Ship of Rio,"
    BB's first pub. music, OUP, *BSB*, p. 21.

270. *Two Part-songs.*
    SATB c./pf., 1933, f.p. London, Ballet Club, 11.xii.33,
        "I Lov'd a Lass," George Wither,
        "Lift Boy," Robert Graves,
    pub. BH, *BSB*, pp. 23, 25.

271. *Venite exultemus Domino.*
    C., org., 1961, pub. pos., FM, 1983,
    BSB, p. 93.

272. *Voices for Today,* Op. 75.
> Anthem on texts by Asoka, Blake, Bright, Camus,
> Hölderlin, Jesus Christ, Lec, Melville, Penn, Shelley,
> Sophocles, Tennyson, Lao Tzu, Virgil, Yevtushenko,
> men's, women's, children's c./org. (ad lib),
> 1965, commissioned for UN 20th anniversary,
> New York, Paris, London, (triple première) 24.x.65,
> pub. FM, *BSB*, p. 103.

273. *Wedding Anthem* ("Amo ergo sum"), Op. 46.
> Ronald Duncan, s./c./org., 1949,
> f.p. London, St. Mark's, N. Audley St., 29.ix.49,
> Lord Harewood's wedding, pub. BH, *BSB*, p. 71.

Unison choral music

274. *Corpus Christi Carol.*
> Anon., u. v./org., (or treble solo), arr. BB from Var. 5,
> "A Boy Was Born," 1961, pub. OUP, *BSB*, p. 93.

275. *Fancie.*
> William Shakespeare, u. v./pf., 1961,
> pub. BH, *BSB*, p. 93.

276. *Friday Afternoons,* Op. 7.
> Twelve children's songs, u. v./pf., 1935,
>> "Begone, Dull Care," "A Tragic Story," "Cuckoo!"
>> "Ee-Oh!" "A New Year Carol,"
>> "I Must Be Married on Sunday,"
>> "There Was a Man of Newington,"
>> "Fishing Song," "The Useful Plough,"
>> "Jazz-Man," There Was a Monkey,"
>> "Old Abram Brown,"
> pub. BH, *BSB*, p. 29.

277. *King Herod and the Cock.*
    U. v./pf., 1965, pub. BH, *BSB*, p. 103.

278. *May.*
    Anon., u. v./pf., 1934, YBP, *BSB*, p. 27.

279. *Pacifist March.*
    Ronald Duncan, u. v./pf., 1937,
    for the Peace Pledge Union, *BSB*, p. 33.

A cappella choral music

280. *Ad majorem Dei gloriam* ("AMDG").
    Gerald Manley Hopkins, seven settings, SATB, 1939,
    pub. FM, 1989, *BSB*, p. 43, *BRI*, p. 297.

281. *Advance Democracy.*
    Randall Swingler, motet, SSAATTBB, 1938, pub. BH,
    (different music from film of same name), *BSB*, p. 143.

282. *Deus in adjutorium meum.*
    Psalm 70, "Haste Thee, O God, to Deliver Me,"
    SATB, 1945, pub. BH, 1983, see citation II.222,
    "This Way to the Tomb," *BSB*, p. 151, *MRL*, p. 1191.

283. *Five Flower Songs,* Op. 47.
    SATB, 1950, f.p. London, BBC, 24.v.51,
        "To Daffodils," Robert Herrick,
        "The Succession of Four Sweet Months," Herrick,
        "Marsh Flowers," George Crabbe,
        "Evening Primrose," John Clare,
        "Ballad of Green Broom," anon.,
    pub. BH, *BSB*, p. 73.

284. *The Holy and the Ivy.*
SATB, 1957, pub. BH, *BSB*, p. 85.

285. *Hymn to St. Cecilia,* Op. 27.
W.H. Auden, SSATB with s., 1942,
f.p. BBC, 22.xi.42, pub. BH,
BSB, p. 51, *BRI, p.* 297.

286. *Phillip's Breeches.*
Charles and Mary Lamb, mixed v., 1936,
BSB, p. 33, *MRL*, pp. 458-460.

287. *Sacred and Profane,* Op. 91.
Eight medieval lyrics, R.T. Davies, ed., SSATB, 1975,
f.p. Snape, 14.ix.75,
"St. Godric's Hymn," "I Mon Waxe Wod,"
"Lenten Is Come," The Long Night,"
"Yif Ic of Luve Can," "Carol,"
"Ye That Pasen By," "A Death,"
pub. FM, *BSB*, p. 123.

Unfinished choral works

288. *Christmas Cantata Sequence.*
V./orch., 1976, inc., *BSB*, p. 125.

289. *Praise We Great Men.*
Edith Sitwell, cantata, v./orch., 1976, inc.,
BSB, pp. 124, 126.

290. *Te Deum.*
C./org., 1961, inc., *BSB*, p. 93.

Solo vocal music

Song-cycles and sets
Various songs

Song-cycles and sets

291. *A Birthday Hansel* ("Seven Burns Songs"), Op. 92.
     Robert Burns, high v./hp., 1975,
     f.p. Cardiff Festival, 19.iii.76,
         "Birthday Song," "Leezie Lindsay,"
         "My Early Walk," "Wee Willie Gray,"
         "My Hoggie," "Afton Water," "The Winter,"
     pub. FM, last four also pub. as *Four Burns Songs,*
     BSB, pp. 122, 125.

292. *Cabaret Songs.*
     W.H. Auden, high v./pf.,
         "Calypso," (1939), "Funeral Blues," (1937),
         "Jam Tart," (1937), "Johnny," (1937)
         "Tell Me the Truth About Love," (1938)
     pub. FM, 1980, *BSB*, pp. 35, 43.

293. *Canticle I, My Beloved Is Mine,* Op. 40.
     Francis Quarles, high v./pf., 1947,
     f.p. London, Central Hall, 1.xi.47,
     pub. BH, *BSB*, p. 65.

294. *Canticle II, Abraham and Isaac,* Op. 51.
     Chester Miracle Play, C/T/pf., 1952,
     f.p. London, Albert Hall, EOG, 21.i.52,
     pub. BH, *BSB*, p. 75.

295. *Canticle III, Still Falls the Rain,* Op. 55.
     Edith Sitwell, T/hn./pf., 1954, f.p. London, WH,
     28.i.55, pub. BH, *BSB*, p. 81.

296. *Prologue, Song and Epilogue.*
     Edith Sitwell, T/pf./hn., 1956, AF, 21.vi.56,
     BSB, p. 83.

297. *Canticle IV, Journey of the Magi,* Op. 86.
     T.S. Eliot, counter T/T/baritone/pf.,
     f.p. AF, 26.vi.71, pub. FM, *BSB*. p. 115.

298. *Canticle V, The Death of Saint Narcissus,* Op. 89.
     T.S. Eliot, T/hp., 1974, f.p. Schloss Elmau, 15.i.75,
     pub. FM, *BSB*, p. 121.

299. *A Charm of Lullabies,* Op. 41.
     Mezzo-soprano/pf., 1947, f.p. The Hague, 3.I.48,
         "A Charm," Thomas Randolph,
         "A Cradle Song," William Blake
         "Come Little Babe," Nicholas Breton, discarded,
         "Highland Ballou," Robert Burns,
         "The Nurse's Song," John Philip,
         "Sephestia's Lullaby," Robert Greene,
         "Somnus," John Denham, discarded,
     pub. BH, *BSB,* p.67.

300. *Five Spiritual Songs* ("Geistliche Lieder").
     J.S. Bach, BB, PP, ed., high v./pf., f.p. AF, 18.vi.69,
         "Gedenke doch, mein Geist, zurücke,"
         "Kommt, Seelen, dieser Tag,"
         "Liebster Herr Jesu," "Komm, süsser Tod,"
         "Bist du bei mir,"
     pub. FM, *BSB*, pp. 110, 111.

301. *The Holy Sonnets of John Donne,* Op. 35.
      High v./pf., f.p. London, WH, 22.xi.45,
        "At the Round Earth's . . ."
        "Batter My Heart," "Death Be Not Proud,"
        "O Might Those Signs," "O My Blacke Soule,"
        "O to Vex Me," "Since She Whom I Loved,"
        "What If This Present," "Thou Hast Made Me,"
        "Perchance for Whom the Bell Tolls," discarded,
      pub. BH, *BSB*, p. 59.

302. *Les illuminations,* Op. 18.
      Arthur Rimbaud, high v./str., 1939,
      f.p., London, 30.i.40,
        "Antique," "Being Beauteous,"
        "Depart," "Fanfare," "Interlude,"
        "Marine," "Parade," "Phrase,"
        "Royauté," "Villes,"
        "Aube," discarded,
      pub. BH, *BSB*, pp. 43, 45, *BRI*, p. 296.

303. *Nocturne,* Op. 60.
      T/seven obligato inst./str., 1958,
      f.p. Leeds, 16.x.58,
        "On a Poet's Lips I Slept," Percy Bysshe Shelley,
        "The Kraken," Alfred, Lord Tennyson,
        "The Wanderings of Cain," Samuel T. Coleridge,
        "Midnight's Bell," Thomas Middleton,
        "But That Night," William Wordsworth,
        "The Kind Ghosts," Wilfred Owen,
        "What Is More Gentle," John Keats,
        "When Most I Wink," William Shakespeare,
      pub. BH, *BSB*, p. 87.

304. *On This Island,* Op. 11.
     W.H. Auden, high v./pf., f.p. London, BBC, 19.xi.37,
     "As it is Plenty," "Let the Florid Music Praise,"
     "Nocturne," "Now the Leaves Are Falling Fast,"
     "Seascape,"
     pub. BH, *BSB,* p. 37.

305. *Our Hunting Fathers,* Op. 8.
     Text devised by W.H. Auden, high v./orch., 1936,
     f.p. Norwich Triennial Festival, 25.ix.36,
     "Rats Away!" "Messalina," "Dance of Death,"
     "Epilogue and Funeral March,"
     pub. BH, *BSB,* p. 31.

306. *Phaedra,* Op. 93.
     Jean Racine, "Phèdre," trans. Robert Lowell,
     dramatic cantata, mezzo-soprano, small orch., 1975,
     f.p. AF, 16.vi.76, pub. FM, *BSB,* pp. 123, 125.

307. *Poet's Echo,* Op. 76.
     Alexander Pushkin, six songs set in Russian,
     high v./pf., Moscow, 2.xii.65,
     pub. FM, *BSB,* p. 103.

308. *Sechs Hölderlin-Fragmente,* Op. 61.
     Johann Christian Friedrich Hölderlin,
     v./pf., f.p. London, BBC, 14.xi.58,
     "Menschenbeifall," "Die Heimat,"
     "Sokrates und Alcibiades," "Die Jugend,"
     "Hälfte des Lebens," "Die Linien des Lebens,"
     pub. BH, *BSB,* p. 87, *KBR,* p. 309.

309. *Serenade,* Op. 31.
    T/hn./str., f.p. London, 15.x.43,
      "Prologue," "Pastoral," John Cotton,
      "Nocturne," Tennyson, "Elegy," William Blake,
      "Dirge," anon., "Hymn," Ben Jonson,
      "Sonnet," John Keats, "Epilogue,"
    pub. BH, *BSB* 57, 152.

310. *Seven Sonnets of Michelangelo,* Op. 22.
    Michaelangelo di Ludovico Buonarroti,
    T/pf., 1940., f. private p. USA, 1940,
    f. public p. London, 23.ix.42,
      Sonnets XVI, XXIV, XXX, XXXI,
      XXXII, XXXVIII, LV, Italian texts,
    pub. BH, *BSB*, p. 45, *KBR*, p. 300.

311. *Songs from the Chinese,* Op. 58.
    Arthur Waley, high v./guitar, 1957, f.p. AF, 17.vi.58,
      "The Autumn Wind," "The Big Chariot,"
      "Dance Song," "Depression,"
      "The Herd-Boy," "The Old Lute,"
    pub. BH, *BSB*, pp. 85, 87.

312. *Songs and Proverbs of William Blake,* Op. 74.
    Baritone/pf., f.p. AF, 24.vi.65,
      "London," "The Chimney-sweeper,"
      "A Poison Tree," "The Tyger,"
      "The Fly," "Ah, Sunflower!"
      "Every Night and Every Morn,"
    pub. FM, *BSB*, pp. 101, 103.

313. *Two Ballads.*

> Vocal duo/pf., f.p. 31.xii.36,
>> "Mother Comfort," Montagu Slater
>> "Underneath the Abject Willow," W.H. Auden,
>> second song set as a solo, <u>ca</u>. 1942,
> see citation II.328, pub. BH, *BSB*, p. 33.

314. *Two Songs.*

> Thomas Lovell Beddoes, v./pf., 1942, f.p. AF, 15.vi.92,
>> "If Thou Wilt Ease Thine Heart,"
>> "Wild With Passion,"
> *BSB*, p. 51.

315. *Who Are These Children?* Op. 84.

> William Soutar, T/pf., 1969, f.p. Edinburgh, 4.v.71,
>> "Who Are These Children?" "A Laddie's Sang,"
>> "A Riddle, the Earth," "A Riddle,"
>> "The Auld Aik," "Bed-time," "Black Day,"
>> "The Children," "The Larky Lad,"
>> "Nightmare," "Slaughter," "Supper,"
>> "Dawtie's Devotion," discarded,
>> "The Gully," "Tradition," both discarded,
> pub. FM, 1972, *BSB*, p. 111.

316. *Winter Words,* Op. 52.

> Thomas Hardy, high v./pf., f.p. Leeds Festival, 8.x.53,
>> "At Day-close in November," "At the Railway
>>> Station, Upway," "Before Life and After,"
>> "The Children," "The Choir Master's Burial,"
>> "If It's Ever Spring Again," "The Little Old Table,"
>> "Midnight on the Great Western," "Sir Nameless,"
>> "Proud Songsters," "Wagtail and Baby,"
> pub. BH, *BSB*, pp. 78, 79, *BRI*, p. 301.

Various songs

317. *Alleluia! Alec's 80th Birthday.*
   Three v., canon on plainchant *'Alleluia'*
   from *Ceremony of Carols*, 1971, for Alec Robertson,
   BSB, p. 117.

318. *Cradle Song.*
   William Blake, v./pf., 1938, *BSB*, p. 39.

319. *Farfield (1928-1930).*
   John Lydgate, v./pf., 1955, *BSB*, p. 81, *MRL*, p. 223.

320. *Fish in the Unruffled Lakes.*
   W.H. Auden, high v./pf., 1938, pub. BH, *BSB*, p. 37.

321. *Night Covers Up the Rigid Land.*
   W.H. Auden, high v/pf., 1937, *BSB*, p.37.

322. *Now Sleeps the Crimson Petal*, C. Matthews, ed.
   Alfred, Lord Tennyson, "Summer Night," T/hn./str.,
   1943, discarded from "Serenade," Op. 31, f.p. 3.iv.87,
   pub. FM, *KBR*, p. 296, *MRL*, p. 1134.

323. *A Poison Tree.*
   William Blake, baritone/pf., 1935,
   see "Songs and Proverbs of William Blake,"
   citation II.312, *BSB*, p. 29.

324. *The Ship of Rio.*
   Walter de la Mare, v./pf., 1963,
   arr. from third of "Three Two-part Songs," 1932,
   see citation II.269, *BSB*, p. 97.

325. *Sleep, My Darling, Sleep.*
     Louis MacNeice, v./pf., 1942,
     BSB, p. 51.

326. *The Sun Shines Down.*
     W.H. Auden, high v./pf., 1937,
     BSB, p. 37.

327. *To Lie Flat on the Back.*
     W.H. Auden, high v./pf., 1937,
     BSB, p. 37

328. *Underneath the Abject Willow.*
     W.H. Auden, v./pf., <u>ca</u>. 1942,
     see citation II.313, *BSB*, p. 49.

329. *O What Is That Sound?*
     W.H. Auden, v./pf., 1942,
     BSB, p. 49.

330. *What's in Your Mind?*
     W.H. Auden, v./pf., 1942,
     BSB, p. 49.

Instrumental music

Music for orchestra
Music for orchestra and soloist
Music for small ensemble
Music for solo instruments
Unfinished works

Music for orchestra

331. *An American Overture,* Op. 27.
     1941, orig. title: *Occasional Overture,* Op. 27,
     wd., pub. FM, 1985, *BSB,* p. 47.

332. *Building of the House,* Op. 79.
     Psalm 127, (v., optional), 1967,
     f.p. AF, ECO, 2.vi.67, pub. FM, see citation II.241,
     BSB, pp. 106, 107.

333. *Canadian Carnival* ("Kermesse Canadian"), Op. 19.
     1939, 6.vi.40, Bristol:, BBC, BH, *BSB,* p. 43.

334. *Mont Juic,* Op. 12.
     A Suite of Catalan Dances, composed jointly with
     Lennox Berkeley. 1937, f.p. London, BBC, 8.i.38,
     pub. BH, *BSB,* p. 37.

335. *Occasional Overture,* Op. 38.
     1946, f.p. BBC, 29.ix.46, wd.,
     pub. FM, 1984, *WLO,* p. 287.

336. *Partita.*
     Chamber orch., 1942, *BSB,* p. 51.

337. *Prelude and Fugue,* Op. 29.
     Str. orch., 1943, f.p. London, Boyd Neel orch.,
     23.vi.43, pub. BH, *BSB*, p. 55.

338. *Simple Symphony,* Op. 4.
     Str. or str. qt., based on BB juvenilia, 1934,
     f.p. Norwich, 6.iii.34, pub. OUP, *BSB*, p. 25.

339. *Sinfonia da requiem,* Op. 20.
     1940, f.p. New York, 30.iii.41,
     pub. BH, *BSB*, pp. 43, 47.

340. *Sinfonietta,* Op. 1.
     Fl./ob./cl./bn./hn./st. qt. or small str. orch., 1932,
     dedicated to Frank Bridge, pub. BH, *BSB*, p. 23.

341. *Suite on English Folk Tunes,* Op. 90.
     "A Time There Was . . . " orch., 1974,
     f.p. AF, ECO, 13.vi.75, pub. FM, *BSB*, p. 123.

342. *Variations on a Theme of Frank Bridge,* Op. 10.
     Str. orch., f.p. Salzburg Festival, Boyd Neel orch.,
     25.viii.37, pub. BH, see citation II.394,
     "Variations for Piano on a Theme of Frank Bridge,"
     BSB, p. 35, *KBR*, p. 293, *MRL*, pp. 498-504.

343. *Variations on Sellinger's Round.*
     Variation IV of VI by British composers, orch., 1953
     f.p. AF, 20.vi.53, *BSB*, p. 77, *BRI*, p. 294.

344. *The Young Person's Guide to the Orchestra,* Op. 34.
     "Variations and Fugue on a Theme of Purcell,"
     orch./speaker, 1946, f.p. Liverpool, 15.x.46,
     pub. BH, see citation II.161, *BSB*, p. 63.

Music for orchestra and soloist

345. *Cadenzas to Haydn's Cello Concerto in C,* Hob. VII b. 1.
    F.p. AF, ECO, 18.vi.64,
    pub. BH, *BSB* 101.

346. *Cadenzas to Mozart's Piano Concerto in E Flat,* K. 482.
    F.p. July, 1966, pub. FM, *BSB,* p. 105.

347. *Concerto in B Minor for Viola, Violin, Orchestra.*
    1932 *BSB,* p. 21.

348. *Diversions for Piano and Orchestra,* Op. 21.
    For left hand, 1940, f.p. Philadelphia, 16.i.42,
    commissioned by Paul Wittgenstein,
    pub. BH, *BSB,* p. 45.

349. *Lachrymae,* Op. 48a.
    Va./str. orch., 1976, adaptation of "Lachrymae, Op. 48,
    see citation II.383, *BSB,* pp. 124, 125.

350. *Piano Concerto No.1 in D,* Op. 13.
    1938, London: BBC Promenade Concert, 18.viii.38,
    BB soloist, pub. BH, *BSB,* p. 39, *BRI,* p. 293.

351. *Scottish Ballad for Two Pianos and Orchestra,* Op. 26.
    1941, f.p. Cincinnati, Bartlett and Robertson, 28.xi.41,
    pub. BH, *BSB,* p. 49, *BRI,* p. 293.

352. *Symphony for Cello and Orchestra,* Op. 68.
    1963, f.p. Moscow, 12.iii.64,
    pub. BH, *BSB*, p. 97.

353. *Violin Concerto,* Op. 15.
    1939, f.p. New York, 28.iii.40,
    pub. BH, *BSB*, p. 43, *BRI*, p. 293.

354. *Young Apollo for Piano and String Orchestra,* Op. 16.
    1939, f.p. Toronto, 2.viii.39, BB soloist,
    wd., pub. FM, 1982, *BSB*, p. 43.

Music for small ensemble

355. *Alla quartetto serioso* ("Go Play, Boy, Play").
    Str. qt., 1933, rev. 1936,
    "Alla burlesca/burlesque,"*
    "Alla marcia/March,"*
    "Alla valse/Waltz,"*
    "March,"*
    "Alla romanza," and "Theme and Variations,"
    (two), inc., *pub. as *Three Divertimenti* (1936),
    and *Alla marcia* (1933), FM, 1983,
    BSB, pp. 23, 25.

356. *Alpine Suite and Scherzo.*
    Recorders, 1955, pub. BH,
    BSB, p. 81, *BRI*, p. 305.

357. *Fanfare for D.W.*
    Brass, 1970, f.p. London, ROH-CG, 30.vi.70,
    "for David Webster," *BSB*, pp. 113, 115.

358. *Fanfare for St. Edmundsbury.*
   Three trpts., 1959, f.p. Cathedral of Bury St. Edmunds,
   Pageant of the Magna Carta, June, 1959,
   pub. BH, *BSB*, p. 89.

359. *Fanfare for S.S. Oriana.*
   Brass, f.p. 3.xi.60, *BSB*, p. 91.

360. *Gemini Variations,* Op. 73.
   Pf./fl./vn., 1965, f.p. AF, Parish Church, 19.vi.65,
   written for Jeney twins, Zoltán and Gabriel,
   quartet for two players, pub. BH, *BSB*, p. 101.

361. *Hankin Booby.*
   Folk dance, wind inst./perc., 1966, f.p. London,
   ECO, 1.iii.67, pub. FM, *BSB*, p. 105.

362. *Phantasy in F Minor.*
   Str. qt., 1932, f.p. London, RCM, 12.xii.32,
   Mendelssohn Scholarship Entry, Cobbett Prize,
   pub. FM, 1983, *BSB*, p. 21.

363. *Phantasy,* Op. 2.
   Ob./vn./va./vc., 1932, f..p. London, 17.ii.33,
   pub. BH, *BSB*, p. 23.

364. *Russian Funeral.*
   Brass/perc., 1936, f.p. London, Westminster Theatre,
   8.ii.36, pub. BH, 1981, *BSB*, p. 31.

365. *String Quartet No. 1 in D,* Op. 25.
   1941, f.p. Los Angeles, 21.ix.41, pub. BH, *BSB*, p. 47.

366. *String Quartet No. 2 in C,* Op. 36.
     1945, f.p. London, 21.xi.45, pub. BH, *BSB*, p. 61.

367. *String Quartet No. 3,* Op. 94.
     1975, f.p. AF, 19.xii.76, pub. FM, *BSB*, p. 125.

Music for solo instruments

Guitar

368. *Nocturnal after John Dowland,* Op. 70.
     Reflections on "Come heavy sleep," 1963,
     f.p. AF, 12.vi.64, pub. FM, *BSB*, p. 99l.

Harp

369. *Harp Suite in C,* Op.83.
     F.p. AF, 24.vi.69, pub. FM, *BSB,* p. 111.

Oboe

370. *Six Metamorphoses after Ovid,* Op. 49.
     Ob., f.p. AF, 14.vi.51, pub. BH, *BSB*, pp. 73, 75.

371. *Temporal Variations.*
     Ob./pf., f.p. London, 15.xii.36,
     pub. FM, 1980, *BSB*, p. 33.

372. *Two Insect Pieces.*
     Ob./pf., 1935, f.p. Manchester, 7.iii.79,
     pub. FM, 1980, *BSB*, p. 29.

Organ

373. *Prelude and Fugue on a Theme of Vittoria.*
F.p. Northampton, 21.ix.46, pub. BH, *BSB*, p. 63.

374. *Theme* (one of four improvised movements for organ).
F.p. London, St. John's, Red Lion Square, 12.xi.36,
BSB, p. 33.

375. *Voluntary* ("Chorale Prelude in D Minor").
1942, *BSB*, p. 51.

Piano or two pianos

376. *Holiday Diary,* Op. 5.
F.p. London, 30.xi.34,
"Early Morning Bathe," "Sailing," "Fun-Fair,"
"Night," pub. BH, *BSB*, p. 27.

377. *Introduction and Rondo alla Burlesca,* Op. 23, No. 1.
Two pf., 1940, f.p. New York, 10.i.41,
pub. BH, *BSB*, p. 45.

378. *Lullaby for a Retired Colonel.*
Two pf., 1936, *BSB*, p. 31.

379. *Mazurka elegiaca,* Op. 23, No. 2.
Two pf., 1941, f.p. New York, pub. BH, *BSB*, p. 47.

380. *Night Piece* ("Notturno").
Pf., 1963, Leeds International Piano Competition,
pub. BH, *BSB*, p. 97.

381. *Sonatina romantica.*
    Pf., 1940, two movements pub. FM, 1986,
    BSB, p. 45.

Timpani

382. *Timpani Piece for Jimmy* (Jimmy Blades).
    Timpani/pf., 1955, *BSB*, p. 81.

Viola

383. *Lachrymae,* Op. 48.
    Va./pf., 1950, f.p. AF, 20.vi.50,
    reflections on a song of John Dowland,
    pub. BH, see citation II.347,
    BSB, pp. 73, 251, *BRI*, p. 304.

Violin

384. *Reveille.*
    Vn./pf., 1937, f.p. London, 23.iv.37,
    pub.FM, 1983, *BSB*, p. 35.

385. *Suite for Violin and Piano,* Op. 6.
    1935, pub.BH, 1977, as
        Three Pieces: March, Lullaby, Waltz,
    BSB, pp. 26, 27, 29, 30, 31, 38.

Violoncello

386. *Cello Sonata in C,* Op. 65.
    1961, f.p. AF, 7.vi.61, pub. BH, *BSB*, p. 23.

387. *Cello Suite No. 1,* Op. 72.
    1964, f.p. AF, 27.vi.65, pub. FM, *BSB*, pp. 101, 103.

388. *Cello Suite No. 2,* Op. 80.
    1967, f.p. AF, 17.vi.68, pub. FM, *BSB*, pp. 107, 109.

389. *Cello Suite No. 3,* Op. 87.
    1971, f.p. AF, 21.xii.74, pub. FM, *BSB*, pp. 115, 123.

390. *Tema-'Sacher'*
    Vc., 1976, f.p. Zurich, 2.v.76, pub. FM, *BSB*, p. 125.

Unfinished works

391. *Ballet on a Basque Scenario.*
    1932, inc., *BSB*, p. 21.

392. *Clarinet Concerto.*
    1942, for Benny Goodman, inc., *BSB*, p. 51.

393. *A Sea Symphony.*
    Orch., 1976, inc., BSB, p. 125.

394. *Variations on a Theme of Frank Bridge.*
    Pf., 1932, theme from Bridge's "Idyll" No. 2,
    for str. qt., inc., see citation II. 342,
    MRL, pp. 241, 502.

395. *Village Organist's Piece.*
    1942, inc., *BSB*, p. 51.

Arrangements and editions

Purcell realizations and editions
Folk song
Various

Purcell realizations and editions

Dramatic works (BB, Imogen Holst, ed.).

396. *Dido and Aeneas.*
        F.p. London, EOG, 1.v.51,
        pub. BH, *BSB*, p. 73, *BRI*, p. 308.

397. *Fairest Isle.*
        C./perc./str. qt., 1937,
        see "Hadrian's Wall" (radio), citation II.195,
        mss. missing, *BSB*, pp. 37, 155.

398. *The Fairy Queen.*
        Purcell, masque (concert version by PP),
        s./mixed c./orch., f.p. AF, 25.vi.67,
        pub. FM, *BSB*, pp. 105, 107, *KBR*, pp. 308-309.

Solo vocal music (BB, PP, ed.).

Harmonia sacra

399. *The Blessed Virgin's Expostulation.*
        High v./pf., 1947, f.p. 15.iv.47,
        pub. BH, *BSB*, p. 65, *KBR*, p. 309.

400. *Job's Curse.*
        High v./pf., 1950, f.p. 3.iii.50,
        pub. BH, *BSB*, p. 73, *KBR*, p. 309.

401. *Saul and the Witch of Endor.*
    S/T/B, s./pf., 1947, f.p. 24.xii.47,
    pub. BH, *BSB*, p. 67, *KBR*, p. 309.

402. *Two Divine Hymns and Alleluia.*
    High v./pf., 1960, f.p. 7.ix.,60,
        "A Morning Hymn," "Alleluia,"
        "In the Black Dismal Dungeon of Despair,"
    pub, BH, *BSB*, p. 91, *KBR*, p. 309.

403. *Three Divine Hymns.*
    High or med. v./pf., 1947, f.p. 24.xii.47,
        "Lord, What is Man?" "We Sing to Him,"
        "Evening Hymn,"
    pub. BH, *BSB*, p. 67, *KBR*, p. 309.

Orpheus Britannicus

404. *Seven Songs.*
    High or med. v./pf., 1947, f.p. 24.i.47,
        "Fairest Isle,"
        "If Music be the Food of Love" (first version),
        "Turn then Thine Eyes," "Music for a While,"
        "Pious Celinda," "I'll sail upon the Dog-star,"
        "On the Brow of Richmond Hill,"
    pub. BH, *BSB*, p. 65, *KBR*, p. 309.

405. *Six Songs.*
    High or med. v./pf., 1948, f.p. 25.iii.48,
        "Mad Bess,"
        "If Music Be the Food of Love" (third version),
        "There's Not a Swain of the Plain,"
        "Not All My Torments,"
        "Man Is for the Woman Made,"
        "Sweeter Than Roses,"
    pub. BH, *BSB*, p. 69, *KBR*, p. 309.

406. *Suite of Songs.*
>> Five songs for high v./orch., 1956, f.p. 3.ii.56,
>>> "Let Sullen Discord Smile,"
>>> "Why Should Men Quarrel,"
>>> "So When the Glittering Queen of Night,"
>>> "Thou Tun'st This World," "'Tis Holiday,"
>> pub. BH, *BSB*, p. 83, *KBR*, p. 309.

407. *Five Songs.*
>> V./pf., 1960,
>>> "I Attempt from Love's Sickness to Fly,"
>>> "I Take No Pleasure," "Hark the Ech'ing Air!"
>>> "Take Not a Woman's Anger Ill,"
>>> "How Blest Are Shepherds,"
>> pub. BH, *BSB*, p. 91, *KBR*, p. 309.

408. *Six Duets.*
>> High and low v./pf., 1961, f.p. 24.v.61,
>>> "Sound the Trumpet,"
>>> "I Spy Celia," "Lost Is My Quiet,"
>>> "What Can We Poor Females Do?"
>>> "No, No, Resistance Is But Vain,"
>>> "Shepherd, Leave Decoying,"
>> pub. BH, *BSB*, p. 93, *KBR*, p. 309.

Various songs by Purcell, (BB, PP, ed.).

409. *The Knotting Song.*
>> V./pf., 1942, *BSB*, p. 51.

410. *The Queen's Epicedium,*
>> "Elegy on the Death of Queen Mary."
>> High v./pf., 1946, f.p. 14.vi.46,
>> pub. BH, *BSB*, p. 61, *KBR*, p. 309.

411. *Sweeter than Roses.*
> V./pf., 1973, *BSB*, p. 290.

412. *When Night Her Purple Veil Had Softly Spread.*
> Secular cantata, baritone/pf., f.p. AF, 24 vi 65,
> pub. FM, *BSB*, pp. 102, 103.

Instrumental music by Purcell (BB, ed.).

413. *The Golden Sonata* ("Trio Sonata in F").
> Two vl./vc./pf., 1945, pub.BH,
> *BRI*, p. 309, *LFL*, pp. 1288, 1289.

414. *Chacony in G minor.*
> Str. qt. or str., 1965, pub. BH, *BSB*, p. 101.

Folk song (BB arr., ed.).

415. *Folk Songs,* Vol. 1 (British Isles).
> High or med. v./pf., 1943, pub. BH,
>> "The Ash Grove," "The Bonny Earl O'Moray,"
>> "Little Sir William," "O Can Ye Sew Cushions?"
>> "The Trees They Grow So High,"
>> "Oliver Cromwell," "The Salley Gardens,"
> *BSB*, p. 55.

416. *Folk Songs,* Vol. 2 (France).
> High or med. v./pf., 1946, pub. BH,
>> "Eho! Eho!" "Fileuse,"
>> "Il est quelqu'un sur terre,"
>> "La belle est au jardin d'amour,"
>> "La noel passee,"
>> "Le roi s'en va-t'en chasse,"
>> "Quand j'etais chez mon pere,"
>> "Voici le printemps,"
> BSB, p. 65.

417. *Folk Songs*, Vol. 3 (British Isles).
    High or med. v./pf., 1947, pub. BH,
      "Come You Not From Newcastle?"
      "The Foggy Foggy Dew,"
      "The Miller of Dee,"
      "O Waly, Waly,"
      "The Plough Boy,"
      "Sweet Polly Oliver,"
      "There's None to Soothe,"
    BSB, p. 67.

418. *Folk Songs,* Vol. 4 (Ireland).
    Moore's Irish Melodies, v./pf., 1960, pub. BH,
      "At the Mid Hour of Night,"
      "Avenging and Bright."
      "Dear Harp of My Country,"
      "How Sweet the Answer,"
      "The Last Rose of Summer,"
      "The Minstrel Boy,"
      "O the Sight Entrancing,"
      "Oft in the Stilly Night,"
      "Rich and Rare,"
      "Sail On, Sail On,"
    BSB, p. 91.

419. *Folk Songs,* Vol. 5 (British Isles).
    V./pf., 1961, pub. BH,
      "The Brisk Young Widow,"
      "Ca' the Yowes,"
      "Early One Morning,"
      "The Lincolnshire Poacher,"
      "Sally in Our Alley,"
    BSB, p. 93.

420. *Folk Songs*, Vol. 6 (England).
  High v./guitar, 1961, pub. BH,
   "Bonny at Morn,"
   "I Will Give My Love an Apple,"
   "Master Kilby,"
   "Sailor-boy,"
   "The Shooting of His Dear,"
   "The Soldier and the Sailor,"
  BSB, p. 95.

421. *Eight Folk Songs* (British Isles).
  Med. v./hp. or pf., 1976, pub. FM,
   "Bird Scarer's Song," "Bonny at Morn,"
   "David of the White Rock,"
   "The False Knight,"
   "I Was Lonely and Forlorn,"
   "Lemady," "Lord, I Married Me a Wife,"
   "She's Like the Swallow,"
  BSB, p. 127.

422. *Heigh-ho! Heigh-hi!* ("Eho! Eho!")
  V./pf., 1945, *BSB*, p. 176, *MRL*, p. 1353.

423. *Tom Bowling.*
  Dibdin, v./pf., 1961, *BSB*, p. 175.

Various stage works, BB arr. and ed.

424. *The Beggar's Opera,* Op. 43.
  John Gay, ballad opera, realized by BB,
  f.p. Cambridge, EOG, 24.v.48,
  rev. 1963, *BSB*, p. 69, *KBR*, p. 308.

425. *Divertimento: Soirées musicales,* Op. 9.
  Rossini, 1936, f.p. New York, American Ballet, 1941,
  Balanchine choreographer, pub. BH, *BSB*, p. 47.

426. *Divertimento: Matinées musicales,* Op. 24.
    Rossini, f.p. New York, American Ballet, 1941,
    Balanchine choreographer, pub. BH, *BSB*, p. 47.

427. *Les sylphides.*
    Fryderyk Chopin, arr. for small orch., 1940,
    New York, Ballet Presentations Inc., Ballet Theatre,
    mss. missing, *BSB*, p. 43.

Sundry settings, BB arr. and ed.

428. *The Holly and the Ivy.*
    SATB, 1957, pub. BH, citation II.284, *BSB,* p. 85.

429. *King Herod and the Cock.*
    1965, un.v./pf., pub. BH, citation II.280, *BSB*, p. 103.

430. *Malayan National Anthem.*
    Military band, 1957, *BSB*, p. 83.

431. *The National Anthem.*
    C./orch.,1961, pub. BH, *BSB*, p. 95.

432. *The National Anthem.*
    Orch., 1971, pub. FM, *BSB*, p. 117.

433. *The Twelve Apostles.*
    T/v./pf., 1962, f.p. AF, 16.v.62, pub. FM, 1981,
    BSB, p. 97.

434. *What the Wild Flowers Tell Me.*
    Mahler, Symphony No. 3, Third movement,
    for reduced orch., 1942, pub. BH, *BSB*, p. 49.

435. *Who Is This in Garments Gory?*
    Arrangement of hymn tune "Ebenezer," v., 1942,
    BSB, p. 49.

PART III

BIBLIOGRAPHY

Structured around six principal groups of citations, the bibliography is selective. It is intended to serve as an introduction to the great amount of analysis, commentary, and descriptive writing generated by authors, critics, and scholars who have focused on Benjamin Britten and his music over the past half-century.

1. **Bibliographies and comprehensive sources**
2. **Biographical and personal studies**
3. **Britten's writings**
4. **Music studies**
5. **Various references**
   Aldeburgh and Glyndebourne
   Histories and dictionaries
   Miscellaneous
6. **University studies**
   Topical index
   Baccalaureate theses
   Master's theses
   Doctoral dissertations

Note on discographies, videos, and audio cassette tapes

The scope of Part III does not extend to lists of audio-visual materials. However, references to discographies which are readily available may be found in several citations, e.g., II.1, 7, 26, 47. Also, the reader is alerted to two especially useful items of general interest to Britten studies:

  (a) a color video tape
  A Time There Was: A Profile of Benjamin Britten, directed by Tony Palmer, with Associate Producer Donald Mitchell (an edited version of a London Weekend Television production, distributed by Kultur International Films [1158], 1980);

  (b) a set of two audio cassette tapes
  Benjamin Britten: The Early Years, 1913-1945, compiled by Donald Mitchell (BBC Study Tapes, Jeffrey Norton Publishers [ECN 201/3], 1984).

Annotation

The annotative process employed here seeks to provide as much pertinent information as can reasonably be culled from the sources cited, letting the authors explain themselves whenever possible.

Group 1

Bibliographies and comprehensive sources

1. Evans, John, Philip Reed, and Paul Wilson, comp.
   A Britten Source Book.
   Aldeburgh: The Britten Estate Limited,
   for The Britten Pears Library, 1987.
   Reprinted, Winchester: St. Paul's Bibliographies, 1988.
   UK distributor: Scolar Press of Gower House,
   Croft Road, Aldershot, Hampshire, GU11 3HR.
   USA distributor: Omnigraphics, Inc., 2400 Penobscot
   Building, Detroit, MI., 48226. 328 p.
   ISBN 0-9511939-2-9. ML 134 .B85 E9.

Chronology (life, works, first performances),	128 p.
Incidental music; catalogue raisonné,	35 p.
Recorded repertoire,	16 p.
Select bibliography (3,273 titles),	126 p.

   The detail and scope of *A Britten Source Book (BSB)* make it a primary resource for Britten studies. Although lacunae were detected in the bibliographic section of the 1987 printing, a reprinting in 1988 remedied the omissions, adding 23 pages of text and more than 400 citations. In the intervening years, further additions and corrections have accumulated, indicating that a second edition would be timely. Regrettably, such a revision appears improbable.

When it first appeared in 1987, *BSB* provided new evidence of Britten's youthful compositional activity, illuminating a prodigious juvenilia and providing fresh insight into his growth and development, especially his early sensitivity to words and his gift for setting the English language. A comprehensive chronology outlines Britten's multi-faceted career as composer, performer, conductor, festival organizer, and publisher. The section titled "The incidental music: a catalogue raisonné" is unique among Britten studies (Philip Reed's PhD dissertation excepted) and includes detailed references to music contributed by Britten to radio, film, and theatre.

Described in the preface as select, *BSB's* bibliography contains 3,273 entries. The bibliography is arranged topically, the organizing principle within topics being chronological rather than alphabetical. The chronological method can be challenging if, for instance, one is searching for a particular author's writing on a particular topic, especially when some of the topics have a hundred or more entries arranged chronologically.

BSB's topics are included here as an indication of the breadth of its bibliography. Of the 178 topics listed in *BSB*, 161 refer to titles of specific compositions. Sixteen of the topical headings refer to persons, institutions, or to types of music. The remaining category is headed "general" and embraces a broad range of topics within its 572 citations. The number of citations found under under each topic or category in *BSB* is given, with an indication of the year(s) covered by the citation(s).

Topics with various titles	Citation(s)	Year(s)
The Aldeburgh Festival	33:	1948-86
Bridge, Frank	9:	1951-79
Britten, Benjamin	124:	1936-86
Pears, Peter	162:	1946-87
Britten-Pears School for Advanced Musical Studies	1:	1980
The English Opera Group	6:	1948-68
Canticles	2:	1960-63
Cello Music	2:	1973-75
Cello Suites	1:	1970
Choral Music	9:	1951-83
Church Music	3:	1939-67
Church Parables	9:	1966-84
Film Music	3:	1950-77
Folksongs	9:	1943-87
Instrumental Music	2:	1949-77
Vocal Music	1:	1967
General (a miscellany of topics–22 p.)	572:	1933-86

Topics with specific music titles

AMDG	1:	1984
Albert Herring	103:	1947-87
Alla Marcia	2:	1983
Alla Quartetto Serioso	1:	1933
Alpine Suite	4:	1956-65
An American Overture	2:	1984-86
Antiphon	2:	1957-65

Ballad of Heroes	7:	1939-73
Ballad of Little Musgrave and Lady Barnard	6:	1944-79
The Beggar's Opera	33:	1948-84
Billy Budd	158:	1949-86
A Birthday Hansel	6:	1976
A Boy was Born	5:	1936-82
The Building of the House	6:	1967-68
The Burning Fiery Furnace	36:	1966-82
Cadenzas: Haydn Cello Concerto in C	1:	1976
Calendar of the Year	1:	1983
Canadian Festival	4:	1940-82
Cantata academica	17:	1959-72
Cantata misericordium	17:	1963-83
Canticle I	8:	1947-87
Canticle II	12:	1952-79
Canticle III	9:	1955-87
Canticle IV	11:	1971-80
Canticle V	9:	1975-76
Cello Sonata	11:	1961-79
Cello Suite No. 1	9:	1965-82
Cello Suite No. 2	6:	1968-69
Cello Suite No. 3	8:	1972-81
Cello Symphony	24:	1963-85
A Ceremony of Carols	4:	1942-74
A Charm of Lullabies	6:	1949-87
Children's Crusade	15:	1969-84
Chorale	2:	1944-61
Coal Face	3:	1946-83
Curlew River	49:	1964-83

Johnson over Jordan	3:	1939-84
Jubilate	1:	1961
Lachrymae	10:	1950-79
Line to the Tschierva Hut	1:	1983
The Little Sweep	42:	1949-84
Love from a Stranger	1:	1983
Mazurka Elegiaca	2:	1941-79
Men of Goodwill	1:	1984
Men of the Alps	1:	1983
A Midsummer Night's Dream	147:	1960-84
Missa brevis	7:	1960-69
Mont Juic	3:	1938-73
Mother Comfort	1:	1938
Night Covers Up the Rigid Land	1:	1987
Night Mail	3:	1936-61
Night Piece	3:	1963-86
Nocturnal	4:	1964-68
Nocturne	14:	1958-87
Noye's Fludde	44:	1958-84
Occasional Overture	1:	1986
On the Frontier	1:	1980
On this Island	4:	1937-81
Our Hunting Fathers	7:	1936-83
Owen Wingrave	62:	1971-84

Sacred and Profane	3:	1975-87
Saint Nicolas	22:	1948-85
Scherzo	2:	1964
Scottish Ballad	5:	1941-52
Sechs Hölderlein-Fragmente	4:	1960-75
Serenade	12:	1944-87
Seven Sonnets of Michelangelo	4:	1941-86
A Shepherd's Carol	1:	1944
Simple Symphony	5:	1938-68
Sinfonia da requiem	22:	1940-87
Sinfonietta	5:	1937-73
Six Metamorphoses after Ovid	5:	1952-67
Soirées musicales	4:	1937-41
Sonatina romantica	1:	1983
Songs and Proverbs of William Blake	11:	1965-69
Songs from the Chinese	2:	1958-59
Spring Symphony	45:	1949-86
String Quartet in D Major (1931)	9:	1975-86
String Quartet No. 1	9:	1941-86
String Quartet No. 2	13:	1943-86
String Quartet No. 3	10:	1976-87
Suite Op. 6	3:	1936-38
Suite on English Folk Tunes	11:	1975-86
The Sword in the Stone	1:	1983
The Sycamore Tree	1:	1968

Review of *A Britten Source Book*.
Patterson, J.L. *Choice*. February 1990, p. 930.

The reviewer notes that "the compilers have succeeded
in their goal to produce the most detailed source of
reference on [Britten's] life and works so far
published." The reviewer observes that "some
undefined abbreviations may not be immediately
recognized by US users; and although a few citations
are from American sources, most cited items are of
British or European origin and would be found only in
large or specialized US libraries." The reviewer
concludes that, despite this and some other limiting
factors, "Britten's international reputation
recommends [*BSB*] to upper-division and graduate
collections."

2. Ford, Boris, comp.
   Benjamin Britten's Poets: the Poetry He Set to Music.
   Manchester: Carcenet Press, 1994. 299 p.
   ISBN 1-85754-022-0. ML 47 .B75.

A misunderstanding led to the printing and publication
of the uncorrected manuscript, resulting in
typographical errors and some misinformation in the
current edition. Notwithstanding this lamentable fact,
Ford's book is an immensely useful volume and is an
essential resource for Britten studies. It reproduces the
poetry and provides brief annotations for most of the
published poetic texts Britten set to music (excepting
those texts used in his operas [see Herbert] and the
church parables). Three indexes give lists of authors,
titles of poems, and first lines. An introduction by the
compiler explores Pears' influence in the choice and
editing of the poetry which Britten set.

3. Foreman, Lewis.
   From Parry to Britten:
   British Music in Letters 1900-1945.
   Portland, Oregon: Amadeus Press, 1987. 332 p.
   ISBN 0-931340-03-9. ML 286.5.F67.

   This anthology of correspondence by Bantock,
   Britten, Delius, Elgar, Balfour Gardiner, Heseltine,
   Moeran, Parry, Stanford, and Vaughan Williams is a
   useful complement to *Letters from a Life: The
   Selected Letters and Diaries of Benjamin Britten
   1913-1976* (Mitchell/Reed, 1991) which focuses
   necessarily on the correspondence from and to
   Benjamin Britten. The scope and content of
   Foreman's anthology serve to give additional
   historical context to aspects of Britten research and
   scholarship, especially to those aspects which focus
   on the earlier years of Britten's life and music.

4. Mitchell, Donald, comp.
   *Benjamin Britten: A Complete Catalogue of His
   Published Works.*
   London: Boosey & Hawkes and Faber Music, 1963.
   Rev. ed. 1973. Reissued with a four page supplement
   "to be inserted between pp. 40 and 41 of 1973 edition,"
   June 1978. 60 p.
   ML 134 .B85 B64.

   A valuable handbook of information on Britten's
   music published up to June 1978. A quantity of
   Britten's juvenilia and some later hitherto unprinted
   works have been published since 1978, potentially
   expanding the 1978 supplement by several pages.
   Contains several indexes and useful performance data.

5. Mitchell, Donald, and Hans Keller, eds.
   *Benjamin Britten: a Commentary on His Works
   from a Group of Specialists.*
   New York: Philosophical Library, 1952. 410 p.
   ISBN 0-837-156238. ML 410 .B835 M5.

The most important early collection of writings on
Britten and his music, including a detailed chronological
catalog of works and a 20-page bibliography—the first
comprehensive listing of bibliographic sources for
Britten studies. Includes:

Georges Auric.	"The Piano Music."
Lennox Berkeley.	"The Light Music."
Joan Chissell.	"The Concertos."
Norman Del Mar.	"The Chamber Operas."
A.E.F. Dickenson.	"The Piano Music."
Paul Hamburger.	"The Pianist."
	"The Chamber Music."
The Earl of Harewood.	"The Man."
Imogen Holst.	"Britten and the Young."
Hans Keller.	"Musical Character."
George Malcolm.	"Purcell Realizations."
	"Dido and Aeneas."
William Mann.	"The Incidental Music."
Donald Mitchell.	"Musical Atmosphere."
Boyd Neel.	"The String Orchestra."
Arthur Oldham.	*"Peter Grimes."*
Peter Pears.	"The Vocal Music."
H.F. Redlich.	"The Choral Music."
Erwin Stein.	*"Billy Budd."*
	"Opera and *Peter Grimes*."
	"The Symphonies."

6. Palmer, Christopher, ed.
   The Britten Companion.
   London: Faber and Faber, 1984. 485 p.
   ISBN 0-571-13168-9. ML 410 .B853.

Thirty-six probing articles and essays, (two contributed
by Britten), a 30-page chronology of works and major
events in the composer's life, a 10-page index of
Britten's music, and notes on the contributors, make
this a valuable resource for Britten studies. Of
particular interest is Donald Mitchell's "What do we
know about Britten now?" which offers an evaluation of
earlier critical and scholarly assessments (<u>ca</u>. 1952) of
the composer, while providing fresh insight born of
Mitchell's long association with Britten and, most
importantly, the surprise of newly discovered or
recently recovered earlier compositions. Includes:

Philip Brett.	"Salvation at Sea: *Billy Budd*."
Benjamin Britten.	"In Conversation with Donald Mitchell."
	"The Composer's Dream."
John Culshaw.	" 'Ben'—A Tribute to Benjamin Britten."
John Evans.	"*Owen Wingrave:* A Case for Pacifism."
	"The Concertos."
Christopher Headington.	"*The Rape of Lucretia*."
Robin Holloway.	"The Church Parables: Limits and Renewals."
Imogen Holst.	"Working for Benjamin Britten. (I)"
	"Entertaining the Young: *The Little Sweep.*"
Graham Johnson.	"Voice and Piano."
Hans Keller.	"*The Beggar's Opera*."

David Matthews.	"The String Quartets and some other Chamber Works."
Wilfrid Mellers.	"*Paul Bunyan*: American Eden."
	"*Turning the Screw*."
	"The Truth of the Dream."
	"Through *Noye's Fludde*."
Anthony Milner.	"The Choral Music."
Donald Mitchell.	"What Do We Know About Britten Now?"
	"Small Victims: *The Golden Vanity, Children's Crusade*."
	"Public and Private in *Gloriana*."
	"Catching On to the Technique in Pagoda-Land."
	"Church Parables: Ritual and Restraint."
	"*Death in Venice*: The Dark Side of Perfection."
	"The Chamber Music: An Introduction."
Christopher Palmer.	"The Ceremony of Innocence."
	"Chaos and Cosmos in *Peter Grimes*."
	"Towards a Genealogy of *Death in Venice*."
	"The Orchestral Song Cycles."
	"Orchestral Works: Britten as Instrumentalist."
Peter Pears.	"On Playing *Peter Grimes*."
Peter Porter.	"Composer and Poet."
Eric Roseberry.	"The Purcell Realizations."
	"The Solo Chamber Music."
Erwin Stein.	"*Albert Herring*."
Rosamund Strode.	"Working for Britten. (II)"

7. Parsons, Charles H., comp.
   A Benjamin Britten Discography.
   Studies in History and Interpretation of Music, vol. 31.
   Dyfed, Wales: Edwin Mellen Press, 1990. 247 p.
   ISBN 0-88946-426-X. ML 156.5 .B74 P4.

An extensive listing of Britten's recorded repertoire to 1990, organized chronologically by date of composition. Page one contains a brief reference to some music of Britten's juvenilia, without explanation. Most of the citations provide detail on the composition and performance aspects of the work, followed by the recording particulars. The detailed information includes:

   a. opus number,
   b. title of work,
   c. author or source of text,
   d. performance forces,
   e. type of work,
   f. dedication,
   g. location and date of first performance,
   h. artists of the first performance,
   i. publisher,
   j. location and date of recording,
   k. recording company and catalog numbers,
   l. number and type of disc,
   m. length of performance time,
   n. producer of the recording,
   o. recording engineer,
   p. author of program notes,
   q. performers of the composition.

8. Reed, Philip.
       "The Incidental Music of Benjamin Britten:
       A Study and Catalogue of His Music for Film,
       Theatre and Radio."
       PhD dissertation, University of East Anglia, 1987.
       3 vols., 703 p. ML 134 .B85 R4.

This extensive study was completed shortly after
Reed and Evans had compiled their catalog of
Britten's incidental music for inclusion in *A Britten
Source Book* (1987). The information found in their
"catalogue raisonné" (pp. 129-165 of *A Britten
Source Book)* will be sufficient for most purposes.
However, the wealth of additional detail in Reed's
dissertation makes it a valuable resource for further
specialized inquiry into the scores, sources, and
performance particulars of Britten's incidental music
composed for broadcast plays, documentary films,
and various stage productions. Three
"perspectives"—one each on the music for film,
theatre, and radio—serve to provide historical
background to the music. Reed notes:

> The present thesis represents the most
> comprehensive study of Britten's Incidental
> Music to date. . . . While it was not feasible to
> scrutinize every incidental music score, a
> compromise has been sought by choosing a
> representative sample from each genre. Details
> of every work, however, may be found in the
> Catalogue of Incidental Music which comprises
> Part IV (preface, p. vi).

9. Rudnick, Tracey.
"Britten-Related Holdings in The Harry Ransom
Humanities Research Center: an Annotated Catalog."
Master of Music Report, The University of Texas,
1992. 90 p.

The Harry Ransom Humanities Research Center at
The University of Texas at Austin contains substantial
Britten-related holdings. The significance of these
holdings may be appreciated by consulting Tracey
Rudnick's very useful Report. Undertaken in response
to a request by Paul Banks of the Britten-Pears
Library for a compilation of all Britten-related
holdings at the center, she describes her research and
the purpose and scope of her Report as follows:

> This project is the beginning of a
> comprehensive catalog that allows more
> complete access to holdings in the Harry
> Ransom Humanities Research Center
> (HRHRC), University of Texas at Austin,
> related to the twentieth-century British
> composer Benjamin Britten (1913-1976). At
> present the HRHRC's catalog lists only direct
> correspondence under the subject heading
> 'Britten.' Not included under that subject
> heading are other relevant materials by artists
> who worked with the composer. These
> materials include libretto manuscripts, letters
> by Britten's collaborators that mention the
> composer, and compositional notebooks
> containing sketches and drafts of several
> composer/author collaborations.

> By relying on the subject heading alone,
> researchers who do not know Britten's life and
> work may overlook several important and
> interesting manuscripts. . . In particular, the
> works of one British collaborator, the English
> poet and playwright Ronald Duncan (1914-
> 1982), have been explored in depth. . . . The
> catalog deals mostly with Duncan's various
> librettos, sketches, and drafts of works for
> which Britten wrote music (p. 1).

The eight chapters comprising this Report include
notes on HRHRC's catalog system and holdings, a
description of Tracey Rudnick's catalog, a catalog of
letters, and a catalog of works. Six appendices make
reference to manuscripts and various tabulations. The
bibliography is useful. Tracey Rudnick's Report does
not include the sizeable archive of correspondence
between Eric Walter White and Britten dating from
the time White was writing his first biography on the
composer—this material and other documentation
being received after Rudnick had completed her
project.

10. Thacker, Martin Nicholas.
     "The Organization of Composer Archives: with
     Special Reference to The Britten-Pears Library,
     Aldeburgh, England."
     Master of Philosophy thesis, The Polytechnic of
     North London, 1986.

     Thacker was Assistant Librarian at the Britten-
     Pears Library (1979-81) where this study was
     conceived. Contains useful information on aspects
     of the Library's early development.

Group 2

```
┌─────────────────────────┐
│      Biographical       │
│          and            │
│    personal studies     │
└─────────────────────────┘
```

11. Blyth, Alan, ed.
    Remembering Britten.
    London: Hutchinson, 1981. 181 p.
    ISBN 0-09-144950-2. ML 410 B853 B6.

An anthology of essays from friends and associates of
the composer. In his preface, Blyth observes:

> My purpose in collecting the memories of those
> who knew the composer best is to preserve the
> first-hand accounts of how a great composer
> lived, worked and behaved. Not surprisingly,
> there are contradictions in these pages (p. 9).

Contributors include:

Sir Frederick Ashton	Dame Janet Baker
Steuart Bedford	Sir Lennox Berkeley
Basil Coleman	Joan Cross
Sir Clifford Curzon	Norman Del Mar
Colin Graham	Keith Grant
Lord Harewood	Imogen Holst
Miss Hudson	Graham Johnson
Hans Keller	Colin Matthews
Donald Mitchell	Sir Peter Pears
Murray Perahia	John Piper

Myfanwy Piper   Mary Potter
Stephen Reiss   Mstislav Rostropovich
Peter Schidlof   William Servaes
Rosamund Strode   Robert Tear
Marion Thorpe   Sir Michael Tippett
Beth (Britten) Welford

12. Britten, Charlotte Elizabeth (Beth) Welford.
My Brother Benjamin.
Bourne End, UK: Kensal Press, 1986. 209 p.
ISBN 0-946041-40-7. ML 410 .B853.

This is a family account of "the way things were,"
written from the perspective of one of Britten's closest
relatives—the younger of his two sisters Barbara and
Elizabeth.

13. Carpenter, Humphrey.
W.H. Auden: A Biography.
Boston: Houghton Mifflin, 1981. 495 p.
ISBN 0-395-30853-4. PS 3501 .U55Z63.

A prelude to the Britten biography which Carpenter
would write in the coming decade. Offers insights into
interactions between Auden and Britten, e.g.

'What immediately struck me,' he [Auden] later
wrote, 'about Britten the composer, was his
extraordinary musical sensitivity in relation to
the English language. . . . Here at last was a
composer who could set the language without
undue distortion.' As to Britten, on the day of
their first meeting he described Auden in his
diary as 'the most amazing man, a very brilliant
and attractive personality' (p. 178).

14. Carpenter, Humphrey.
    Benjamin Britten: A Biography.
    New York: Charles Scribner, 1993. 677 p.
    ISBN 0-684-19569-0. ML 410 .B853 C37.

A biographical *tour de force*! It is not, however, the 'official' life, the writing of which Britten, prior to his death, had assigned to his long-time friend and publisher, Donald Mitchell. Mitchell had prepared an outline model for such a biography, but when he undertook the task of compiling the multi-volume series *Letters from a Life* [Mitchell/Reed, 1991], Carpenter indicated his eagerness to write the long-awaited biography and Mitchell accorded him full cooperation. Nevertheless, the work remained Carpenter's sole responsibility. Treating his subject somewhat sensationally, Carpenter utilizes what reviewer David Blum describes as "speculative erotic analysis" in an endeavor to connect Britten's perceived sexual complexes with his presumed creative processes. Carpenter concludes his Preface: "I should emphasize that this portrait of Britten and interpretation of his music represent solely my own viewpoint" (p. x).

Reviews:
(a) Blum, David. *"Sex, Triads and Chromaticism."*
    New York Times Book Review,
    July 11, 1993, p. 9.
(b) Holloway, Robin. "Strange Victory."
    The Times Literary Supplement,
    November 13, 1992. pp. 5-6.
(c) Rorem, Ned. "Composer on a Grand Scale."
    Washington Post, Book World,
    June 20, 1993, p. 8.

15. Duncan, Ronald.
    Working with Britten; A Personal Memoir.
    Bideford, Devon: Rebel Press, 1981. 173 p.
    ISBN 0-900615-30-3. ML 410 .B853.

    An assessment of four decades of close association
    with Britten by a poet who wrote ". . . what I knew
    about him as a man is at its best, biography—at its
    worst, gossip. But I can describe what it was like
    working and writing for him" (p. 9).

16. Elliott, Graham John.
    "Benjamin Britten: The Things Spiritual."
    PhD dissertation, University of Wales, 1985. 212 p.
    ML 410 .B853 E45.

    Elliott addresses dimensions of the composer's
    character which, by and large, receive less than
    adequate treatment from most of Britten's
    biographers. He notes in his opening summary
    statement:

    > It has been suggested that Britten felt
    > himself to be outside 'normal' society, and
    > that this accounts for his obvious sympathy
    > for the outsider in his operas. Although this
    > is undoubtedly an important aspect of
    > Britten's total make-up, the present thesis
    > seeks to show that he was concerned with
    > very much more universal concerns, which
    > are frequently to be seen as having a strong
    > spiritual dimension (p. i).

    See also Elliott's article "The Operas of Benjamin
    Britten: A Spiritual View," in *The Opera Quarterly,*
    4-3 (Autumn, 1986): 29-44.

17. Gishford, Anthony, ed.
   Tribute to Benjamin Britten on his Fiftieth Birthday.
   London: Faber and Faber, 1963. 196 p.
   ML 55 .B75 G6.

A 'Festschrift' of twenty-seven birthday tributes to Britten. Personal reminiscences from some of the composer's friends, as well as articles from Britten's contemporaries—musicians, poets, artists, and those who collaborated with the composer in his performances and productions. Includes:

Julian Bream.   "The Morley Consort Lessons."
Kenneth Clark.   "The Other Side of the Alde."
Aaron Copland.   "A Visit to Snape."
Joan Cross.   "The Bad Old Days."
Clifford Curzon.   "Twenty Years Ago."
Ronald Duncan.   "The Humanity of George Crabbe."
The Earl of Cranbrook.   "The Suffolk Countryside."
The Earl of Harewood.   "In Memoriam: Erwin Stein
                            1885-1958."
E.M. Forster.   "Arctic Summer."
R. Gathorne-Hardy. "Capriccio: Lathyrus Maritimus."
Anthony Gishford.   "The Peaceable Kingdom."
Carlo M. Giulini.   "Excerpt from a Letter to the
                            Editor."
Imogen Holst.   "Indian Music."
Hans Keller.   "Key Characteristics."
Ludwig Prince of
Hesse and the Rhine.   "Ausflug Ost 1956."
George Malcolm.   "Boys' Voices."
Elizabeth Mayer.   "A Poem by Goethe."

Yehudi Menuhin.   "A Chivalrous Tradition."
Donald Mitchell.   "The Truth About Cossi."
Peter Pears.   "Some Notes on Translation of
                         Bach's Passions."
Myfanwy Piper.   "Some Thoughts on the Libretto
                         of *The Turn of the Screw.*"
William Plommer.   "Edward Fitzgerald."
Francis Poulenc.   "Hommage à Benjamin Britten
Mstislav Rostropovich.   "Dear Ben. . . "
Paul Sacher.   "Dinu Lipatti."
Edith Sitwell.   "Praise We Great Men."
Eric Walter White. "Greek Shadow Theatre."

18. Godfrey, Paul.
   Once in a While the Odd Thing Happens.
   London: Methuen Drama, 1990. 86 p.
   ISBN 0-413-64480-4. PR 6057 .0447 06.

A play in three acts, commissioned by The National
Theatre Studio and first presented in 1990. Set in
England and America between the late 1930s and
1945, its cast of characters include Britten, Pears,
Auden, Beth Britten, and Beata Mayer. While not
intended as a "biographical play," the book throws
illuminating shafts of insight on the life and character
of Britten and his friends and is worth perusing. From
the author's foreword:

> The play is a fiction but I have portrayed the
> characters as I belive they were and shown
> events as I understand them. The purpose was
> not to do a biographical drama but to use these
> specific figures to create a play with the widest
> resonance. . . .The title is a chorus from the
> Britten/Auden American operetta *Paul Bunyan.*

19. Headington, Christopher.
    Britten.
    London: Eyre Methuen, 1981. 166 p.
    ISBN 0-8419-0803-6. ML 410 .B853 H4.

    A useful biographical study which draws, as the
    author notes, "upon the generous help of a number of
    people who talked to me about Benjamin Britten, . . .
    These include The Very Revd Dr Walter Hussey,
    Lord and Lady Redcliffe-Maud, Mrs Beth Welford
    and Sir Lennox Berkeley. . . ." (p. vii). In fact, Sir
    Lennox provides personal insights into Britten's work
    ethic in a preface to the study where he states:

    > This book tells the story of Britten's life, not by
    > separating the life from the music, but by treating
    > the two things concurrently. I feel that the author
    > was right in doing so as Britten's life was very
    > much bound up with his work, indeed one could
    > say that his life was his work. He had a strong
    > sense of his vocation as a composer and would
    > allow nothing to interfere with it (p. ix).

20. Headington, Christopher.
    Peter Pears.
    London: Faber and Faber, 1993. 351 p.
    ISBN 0-571-17072-2. ML 420 .P37 H42.

    Commissioned by Donald Mitchell and his fellow
    executors, this official biography of Pears is an
    essential complement to the biographies of Benjamin
    Britten. It is reviewed positively by Robin Holloway
    in a concurrent review of Humphrey Carpenter's
    Benjamin Britten: A Biography, 1991, and of
    Headington's *Peter Pears* (see citation III.14).

21. HRH The Princess of Hesse and the Rhine.
    Dear Friends (1956-1986).
    Edward Mace, comp., 1988. Privately published.
    56 p. Copy located in The Britten-Pears Library,
    Aldeburgh, UK.

From the introduction by Mace:

> In 1956 the Princess of Hesse and the Rhine
> began the amiable habit of recording her travels
> in the form of open letters to her friends. The
> original letters were posted to Wolfsgarten and
> her neice, Princess Beatrix of Hohenlohe, had
> them copied, exactly as they were written, and
> distributed to friends all over the world. They
> always opened in the same way, 'Dear Friends.'
> Hence the title of this collection. But the two
> simple words have a deeper significance because
> of the extracts, chosen from nearly a million
> words, revolve around four people, her husband
> Prince Ludwig, Benjamin Britten and Peter Pears
> (p. 3).

The letter which concludes this collection is a
poignant account of the composer's death and of the
days leading to that event. This letter also provides
glimpses of how Britten was viewed by his closest
friends—a deeply religious man, characterized by
humility, compassion, hatred of war and power, warm
friendship and capacity for loving, possessing integrity
as man and musician, caring for the underdog,
kindness and sympathy, and a glorious sense of
humour.

22. Holst, Imogen.
    Britten.
    3rd ed. London: Faber and Faber, 1980. 96 p.
    ISBN 0-571-18000-0. ML 410 .B853.

    Imogen Holst wrote her biography of Britten from
    direct, personal experience as the composer's assistant
    for 24 years. Her study also reflects those special
    qualities which only a sympathetic fellow artist—her
    father was Gustav Holst and she was herself a
    musician of considerable ability and talent—could
    bestow on the narration of events in the life of this
    composer. A sensitive and perceptive study.

23. Hurd, Michael.
    Benjamin Britten.
    London: Novello, 1966. 22 p.
    ML 410 .B853 H9.

    A brief study of Britten's life and music up to 1966.

24. Kendall, Alan.
    Benjamin Britten.
    London: Macmillan, 1973. 112 p.
    SBN 333-15226-3. ML 410 .B853 K4.

    Yehudi Menuhin, in a sympathetic introduction to this
    study celebrating Britten at sixty, writes: "A lone and
    supremely sensitive sounding-board, he does not
    pronounce or indulge himself in the manner of the
    romantic, nor of the didactic[,] neither buccaneer,
    schoolmaster, nor academic, but reserves himself for
    that which he chooses to allow to play upon him. . .
    [BB] . . . has retained a youthfulness, a perennial
    innocence and that idealistic passion that is so rare."

25. Kennedy, Michael.
    Portrait of Walton.
    Oxford: Oxford University Press, 1990. 348 p.
    ISBN 0-19-282774-X. ML 410 .W292 K4.

    Contains numerous references to Britten, including Sir
    William Walton's views of his younger contemporary
    and exchanges of correspondence which reveal a
    warm friendship between the two composers.

26. Kennedy, Michael.
    Britten.
    Rev. ed. London: J.M. Dent, 1993. 355 p.
    ISBN 0-460-86077-1. ML 410 .B853 K45.

    An excellent introduction to Britten by an astute, but
    compassionate critic of twentieth-century music and
    musicians. Includes a list of works, a discography,
    and a seventy-person 'personalia.' Kennedy notes:

    > I belong to the generation which witnessed
    > Benjamin Britten's career from its meteoric
    > early brilliance to the courageous last years of
    > struggle against illness. His music was an
    > essential part of our lives, a continuous
    > counterpoint to all the other activities of the
    > crowded years. Each new work was a
    > landmark. Some of them were easy to accept
    > from the outset; others were perhaps underrated
    > or misunderstood. I have written this book
    > partly in expiation of my own
    > misunderstandings at certain periods, but
    > mainly as a celebration of the joy his music has
    > brought me for over forty years (p.v).

27. Mason, Colin, ed.
    "Britten at Fifty."
    In: *Tempo, A Quarterly Review of Modern Music,*
    vols. 66-67 (1963): 64 p.

    This special birthday issue of *Tempo*, devoted almost
    wholly to Britten and his music, contains eight articles
    from authors John Andrewes, Peter Evans, Hans
    Keller, Donald Mitchell, Anthony Payne, Eric
    Roseberry, John Warrack, and Fanny Waterman.

28. Mitchell, Donald.
    Britten & Auden in the Thirties: The Year 1936.
    Seattle: University of Washington Press, 1981. 176 p.
    ISBN 0-295-95814-6. ML 410 .B853 M6.

    Mitchell looks at a "key year" in Britten's
    development. A penetrating and pioneering study.

29. Mitchell, Donald.
    "Outline Model for a Biography of Benjamin Britten
    (1913-1976)." In *Festschrift Albi Rosenthal*
    (Tutzing: Hans Schneider, 1984), pp. 239-251.
    ISBN 3-7952-0432-1.

    An essay, including an introductory paragraph
    alluding to the rôle played by Albi Rosenthal (whose
    70th birthday this *Festschrift* celebrates) in the
    development of the Britten-Pears Library and Archive
    in Aldeburgh. The style, scope and sweep of
    Mitchell's 'outline' are such as makes one wish that
    he had indeed found time to fulfill the commission
    Britten assigned him—that of official biographer.
    Letters from a Life (Mitchell/Reed, 1991), when
    completed, may eventually satisfy that wish.

30. Mitchell, Donald, and John Evans.
Benjamin Britten 1913-1976: Pictures from a Life.
London: Faber and Faber, 1978. 456 p.
ISBN 0-684-15974-0. ML 410 .B853.

Described as "A Pictorial Biography," this study
serves as a photographic complement to the later
Letters from a Life (Mitchell/Reed, 1991). Taken
together, *Letters* and *Pictures* provide a well-
rounded and finely detailed portrait of Britten.

31. Mitchell, Donald, and Philip Reed., eds.
*Letters from a Life: The Selected Letters
and Diaries of Benjamin Britten 1913-1976.*
Berkeley: University of California Press, 1991.
Vol. I, 1923-1939; 619 p. Vol. II, 1939-1945, 784 p.
(Vols. III, IV, V in preparation in 1996.)
ISBN 0-520-06520-4. ML 410 .B853 A4.

Vols. I, II include:
　Index of correspondents.
　Index of works.
　Introduction by Donald Mitchell, 65 p.,
　　contains essays on Britten's life, diaries,
　　letters, family, relationship with Pears.
　Chronologies.
　Letters and Diaries 1923-1945:
　　　1923-30, childhood and schooldays:
　　　　　South Lodge and Greshams;
　　　1930-33, college years;
　　　1934-39, a working life;
　　　1939-42, the American years;
　　　1942-45, the return to England:
　　　　　the writing of *Grimes*.

This projected sequence of books comprises the most ambitious, detailed, and comprehensive study of Benjamin Britten conceived thus far. Commentators have noted that, when completed, this five-volume series, replete with their copious annotations, footnotes, and extensive cross-references, *Letters from a Life* will constitute what virtually amounts to an autobiography, though unintended by the composer, as well as the long-awaited full-dress and official biography of Britten.

As Britten's biographer of choice, Mitchell was well positioned to fulfill his commission. Although his original concept was not realized, *Letters from a Life* far exceeds the limits of the usual biographical study, providing a depth, breadth, and richness of perspective concerning the composer, his associates, and his times available from no other published source. An indispensable biographical reference.

Reviews:

(a) Adams, Byron. *"Letters from a Life: Selected Letters and Diaries of Benjamin Britten."* Notes, Vol. 49, Book Reviews. June 8, 1993, pp. 1406-8.

(b) Driver, Paul. "Britten's Life—with Grace Notes." *Financial Times Weekend,* Books. June 15/16, 1991, p. XVI.

(c) Osborne, Charles. "Scoring High on Haircuts." *Weekend Telegraph,* Books. Saturday, June 15, 1991, p. XVII.

32. Reed, Philip, ed.
    The Travel Diaries of Peter Pears, 1936-1978.
    Aldeburgh: The Britten-Pears Library in conjunction
    with The Boydell Press, Woodbridge, 1995. 242 p.
    (Issued as an item in the Aldeburgh Studies in Music.)
    ISBN 0-85115-364-X.

    Twelve chapters cover Pears' travels in various
    countries on different occasions, ranging from his
    "American Tour with the New English Singers" in
    1936, to his appearances in New York in 1974 (*Death
    in Venice*) and again in 1976 (*Billy Budd*). Includes
    illustrations and a sizeable 'personalia.'

33. Reed, Philip, ed.
    *On Mahler and Britten: Essays in honour of
    Donald Mitchell on his 70th birthday.*
    (Aldeburgh: The Britten-Pears Library in conjunction)
    with The Boydell Press, Woodbridge, 1995. 355 p.
    Issued as an item in the Aldeburgh Studies in Music.
    ISBN 0-85115-382-8. ML 410 .M23 O5.

    This substantial 'Festschrift' includes a Donald
    Mitchell chronology and an extensive bibliography of
    Mitchell's writings (1945-1995). The main text
    devotes 13 chapters to Mahler and 15 to Britten, the
    latter adding significantly to the literature on the
    composer and his contemporaries.

34. Schaffer, Murray.
    British Composers in Interview.
    London: Faber and Faber, 1963. 187 p.
    ML 390 13B.

    Interview ten is with Britten (pp. 113-24).

35. Schellinger, Paul E., ed.
    St. James Guide to Biography.
    London: St. James Press, 1991. pp. 86-7
    ISBN 1-55862-146-6. CT 101 .S7.

    Patricia Howard comments on studies of Britten by
    Alan Blyth, Beth Britten, Imogen Holst, Michael
    Kennedy, Donald Mitchell, and Eric Walter White.

36. Seebohm, Caroline (Mrs Walter Lippincott).
    Conscripts to an Age: British Expatriates 1939-1945.
    Draft manuscript of unpublished article in The Britten-
    Pears Library, n.d. (attached letter dated 31.v.83): 45 p.

    Provides insight into the cultural climate of the years
    immediately prior to the outbreak of World War II
    and of the impact of the gathering storm on the
    younger generation of artists, including Britten. An
    extract gives the flavor of the writing.

    > Composers in general were regarded with less
    > than respect in England. 'At a tennis party in
    > my youth,' Britten related later, 'I was asked
    > what I was going to do when I grew up—what
    > job I was aiming at. "I am going to be a
    > composer," I said. "Yes, but what else?" was
    > the answer.' So, like many artists frustrated in
    > their own country, he was desperate for a new
    > environment in which to work. He was a
    > 'discouraged young composer—muddled, fed
    > up and looking for work, longing to be used.'
    > He met Aaron Copland in 1938, and the two
    > musicians immediately got on famously; the
    > American no doubt indicating the possibilities
    > available for composers in his country (p. 3).

37. Thorpe, Marion, ed.
    Peter Pears: A Tribute on His 75th Birthday.
    London: Faber Music, in association with
    The Britten Estate, The Red House, Aldeburgh,
    Suffolk, 1985. 145 p.
    ISBN 0-571-10063-5. ML 420 .P3.

Led by HM Queen Elizabeth The Queen Mother, this distinguished assembly of friends offers some special and memorable anecdote, insight, or message to honor the life and artistry of Britten's life companion and professional colleague Sir Peter Pears. The comments inevitably cast direct and indirect illumination upon aspects of the composer himself. The contributors to this 'Festschrift" constitute a study in personalia associated with both Britten and Pears.

HM Queen Elizabeth The Queen Mother
Dame Janet Baker   Steuart Bedford
George Behrend   Sir Lennox Berkeley
Peter Bowring   William Burrell
Jill Burrows   Alan Bush
Richard Butt   Joan and Isador Caplan
Basil Coleman   Aaron Copland
The Dowager Countess of Cranbrook
Joan Cross   Gordon Crosse
Eric Crozier   Hugues Cuénod
Jeremy Cullum   David Drew
Bettina Ehrlich   Osian Ellis
John Evans   Nancy Evans
Dietrich Fischer-Dieskau   Jill Gomez
Colin Graham   Vlado Habunek
The Earl of Harewood   Heather Harper
Hans Werner Henze

HRH The Princess of Hesse and the Rhine
Derek Hill   Barbara Holmes
The Very Reverend Walter Hussey
Graham Johnson   Hans Keller
Oliver Knussen   Bob and Doris Ling
Hans Ludwig   Witold Lutoslawski
Neil Mackie   Hugh Maguire
Lucie Manén   Colin Matthews
Tony Meyer   Yehudi Menuhin
Sieglinde Mesirca   Donald Mitchell
Henry Moore   Murray Perahia
Sue Phipps   John Piper
Priaulx Rainier   Stephen Reiss
Mstislav Rostropovich and Galina Vishnevskaya
Paul Sacher   Norman Scarfe
Elisabeth Legge-Schwarzkopf
William Servaes
Peter Stansky and William Abrahams
Rosamund Strode   Marshall B. Sutton
Frank Taplin   Rita Thomson
Marion Thorpe   Sir Michael Tippett
Theodor Uppman   Fanny Waterman
Beth Welford   Sir John Willis
Paul Wilson and the Staff of the Britten-Pears Library
                    Anne Wood

The book concludes with excerpts from the personal
diaries of Benjamin Britten for 1937 and 1938;
several photographs of Pears in performance poses; a
list of operatic appearances with a prefatory note by
Harold Rosenthal; a list of first performances by
Pears; and a discography of Pears' recorded
repertoire.

38. White, Eric Walter, ed. by John Evans.
    Benjamin Britten: His Life and Operas.
    2nd ed. Berkeley: University of California Press,
    1983. 322 p.
    ISBN 0 520 04894. ML 410 .B853 W4.

White was Britten's first biographer. His study
Benjamin Britten: eine skizze von Leben und Werk,
was published in Zurich by Bettina and Martin
Hurlimann, with an English translation appearing in
November 1948. Revised editions were issued in
1954 and again in 1970. The current (1983) edition,
described as the "second" in the preface by White,
contains the following statement:

> I am deeply grateful to John Evans, Research
> Scholar to The Britten Estate, who has
> undertaken the editorial responsibility for the
> present edition. He has incorporated my new
> chapters on *Owen Wingrave* and *Death in
> Venice*, has updated the bibliography and list of
> published works, and has revised the text,
> where recent scholarship has shed new light on
> aspects of Britten's career (p. 16).

39. Young, Percy M.
    Britten.
    London: Ernest Benn, 1966. 68 p.
    ML 3930 .B83.

A concise introduction to some essential aspects of
Britten's background, local and regional influences,
his relationship to English music, his development as a
composer, his emergence on the international musical
stage, and his work for young people.

Group 3

Britten's writings

Generally diffident about expressing his opinions and views on musical and other subjects through the medium of language and the printed page (feeling himself less sure in this mode of expression and much more secure when conveying his thought via the vehicle of music), Britten, nevertheless, has left us a generous sheaf of writings which further contribute to a full and rounded picture of his life and times. *A Britten Source Book* (Evans/Reed/Wilson, 1987) contains some 124 citations of Britten's published writings that appeared over a half century between the years 1936 and 1986. A substantial number of the composer's sallies into journalism took the form of contributions to the annual Aldeburgh Festival Programme Books (AFPB)—"a rich source for Britten studies," as the foreword to the revised bibliography in *A Britten Source Book* observes.

A highly selective approach has been adopted here by which to introduce the reader to a brief sampling of significant writing by Britten, with the expectation that *BSB*'s bibliography will be consulted for a more complete investigation of the composer's articles and other writings. This note would be incomplete without reference to the body of Britten's published correspondence which has appeared in the volumes *Letters from a Life: The Selected Letters and Diaries of Benjamin Britten 1913-1976* (Mitchell/Reed, 1991).

40. Britten, Benjamin.
    "How I Became a Composer."
    In: *The Radio Listener's Weekend Book,*
    ed. John Pringle (London: Odhams, n.d.), pp. 108-112.

A print version of a broadcast talk which Britten gave
to Sixth Forms (English school system). Affords a
glimpse of the composer from a perspective that is all
too rare—namely the 'how-to-get-started' point of
view of the expert shared with a young audience. (*BSB*
p. 197, cites an article of similar title: "How to
Become a Composer." In: *Listener* [London: BBC,
November 7, 1942].) A quotation illustrates one of
Britten's major contentions—the value of technique.

> . . . . I cannot overestimate this importance of
> technique. It is the same in every walk of life. It
> is no good having ideas unless you can carry
> them out. In tennis you may have a superb
> scheme for bringing your opponent up to the net
> and then lobbing over his head, but this scheme
> is useless unless you can make drop-shots and
> lobs. Obviously it is no use having a technique
> unless you have the ideas to use this technique;
> but there is, unfortunately, a tendency in many
> quarters today to believe that brilliance of
> technique is a danger rather than a help. This is
> sheer nonsense. There has never been a
> composer worth his salt who has not had
> supreme technique. I will go further than this
> and say that in the work of your supreme artists
> you cannot separate inspiration from technique
> (p. 111).

41. Britten, Benjamin.
     On Receiving the First Aspen Award.
     London: Faber and Faber, 1964. 23 p.
     Reprinted by Faber Music in association with
     Faber and Faber, 1978.
     ISBN 0-57110023-6. ML 60 .B864 O5.

Benjamin Britten was chosen from among more than a
hundred artists, scholars, writers, poets, philosophers,
and statesmen nominated by leaders in intellectual and
cultural fields throughout the world to be the first
recipient of The Robert O. Anderson Aspen Award
established in 1963 to honour "the individual
anywhere in the world judged to have made the
greatest contribution to the advancement of the
humanities."

The citation read:

> **To Benjamin Britten**
> **who, as a brilliant composer, performer,**
> **and interpreter through music of human**
> **feelings, moods, and thoughts, has truly**
> **inspired man to understand, clarify and**
> **appreciate more fully his own nature,**
> **purpose and destiny.**

This text of Britten's acceptance speech "On
Receiving the First Aspen Award" is a lucid statement
of his artistic credo and provides insight into his
humanity and personal motivation as a composer.

42. Britten, Benjamin, with Imogen Holst.
   The Wonderful World of Music.
   London: MacDonald, 1968. 70 p.
   A reissue of the version titled *The Story of Music.*
   London: Rathbone Books, 1958.
   ML 160 .B863 W6.

43. Britten, Benjamin.
   "On Behalf of Gustav Mahler."
   In: *Tempo*, ed. Donald Mitchell, (March, 1977): pp.
   14-15. First published in the independent American
   series of *Tempo*, February, 1942, 2-2.

   Written when Britten was finishing an orchestral
   reworking of the third movement of Mahler's Third
   Symphony. He recounts his youthful introduction to
   the music of Mahler, his surprise at what he heard,
   and the beginning of his life-long commitment to the
   promotion of the composer.

44. Britten, Benjamin.
   "On *Oedipus Rex* and *Lady Macbeth.*"
   In: *Tempo*, ed. Donald Mitchell, (March, 1977):
   pp. 10-12.

   In a prefatory note, Donald Mitchell describes the
   genesis of this brief, but important sample of musical
   criticism by Britten who rarely appeared in the rôle of
   public music critic and for whom this aspect of music
   journalism was usually anathema. The piece was
   commissioned for the first issue of *World Film News*
   and was written in 1936.

Group 4

Music studies

45. Banfield, Stephen.
    Sensibility and English Song:
    Critical Studies of the Early 20th Century.
    Cambridge University Press, 1985. 619 p.
    ISBN 0-521-37944-X. ML 2831 .B35.

    Britten's contribution to the literature of twentieth-
    century song is given sensitive consideration in a
    section entitled "Rethinking the Voice II."

46. Banks, Paul, ed.
    Britten's Gloriana: Essays and Sources.
    Woodbridge, UK: Boydell and Brewer,
    in conjunction with The Britten-Pears Library.
    Aldeburgh, 1993. 193 p.
    ISBN 0-85115-340-2. ML 410 .B853 B75.

    A collection of critical studies resulting from a course
    on *Gloriana* given at the Britten-Pears School for
    Advanced Musical Studies at Snape in 1991. Includes:

Paul Banks and Rosamund Strode.	"Gloriana: A List of Sources."
Peter Evans.	"The Number Principle and Dramatic Momentum in *Gloriana*."
Robert Hewison.	"'Happy Were He': The *Gloriana* Story."

Antonia Malloy.	"Britten's Major Set-Back? Aspects of the First Critical Response to *Gloriana.*"
Donald Mitchell.	"The Paradox of *Gloriana*: Simple and Difficult."
Philip Reed.	"The Creative Evolution of *Gloriana.*"
Antonia Malloy.	"Gloriana: A Bibliography."

The concluding paragraph to the preface by Paul Banks is instructive:

> The idea of publishing papers from a Britten-Pears School study course had been mooted in the past, . . . with this volume a series is launched which it is hoped will reflect in diverse ways the astonishing musical heritage, extensive archival resources and vibrant musical life of Aldeburgh and, more broadly, East Anglia. Much of that richness has its roots in the lives of three outstanding musicians—Benjamin Britten, Peter Pears and Imogen Holst—and it is inevitable that the pre-eminence of their contribution will be reflected in the series. But not exclusively. A new generation of composers and performers is now heard in Aldeburgh, new music education projects are promoted by the Aldeburgh Foundation and the libraries—the Britten-Pears Library in Aldeburgh, and the Holst Library at Snape—have collections which extend into unexpected repertoires. The series will try to encompass this diversity (p. vii).

47. Brett, Philip, comp.
   Benjamin Britten: Peter Grimes.
   Cambridge: Cambridge University Press, 1983. 217 p.
   ISBN 0-521-29716-8. ML 410 .B853 B45.

One in a series of opera studies which intends to
address "the genesis of the work, its sources or its
relation to literary prototypes, the collaboration
between librettist and composer, and the first
performance and subsequent stage history. A final
section gives a select bibliography, a discography, and
guides to other sources" (p. v). Includes:

Philip Brett.	"'Fiery Visions' (and Revisions): Peter Grimes in Progress."
	"Breaking the Ice for British Opera: Peter Grimes on Stage."
	"Britten and Grimes."
	"Postscript."
Benjamin Britten.	"Introduction."
E.M. Forster.	"Two Essays on Crabbe."
J.W. Garbutt.	"Music and Motive: Peter Grimes."
Peter Garvie.	"Plausible Darkness: Peter Grimes After a Quarter of a Century."
Hans Keller.	"Peter Grimes: the Story, the Music Not Excluded."
David Matthews.	"Act II Scene 1: An Examination of the Music."
Donald Mitchell.	"Montagu Slater (1902-1956): Who Was He?"
Peter Pears.	"Neither a Hero Nor a Villain."
Desmond Shaw-Taylor.	"Peter Grimes: a Review of the First Performance."
Edmond Wilson.	"An account of Peter Grimes from 'London in Midsummer'"

48. Cooke, Mervyn, and Philip Reed.
    Benjamin Britten: Billy Budd.
    Cambridge: Cambridge University Press, 1993. 180 p.
    ISBN 0-521-38750-7. ML 410 .B853 C7.

    Includes:
    Mervyn Cooke. "Synopsis Herman Melville's
                    Billy Budd."
                    "Britten's *Billy Budd*: Melville as
                        Opera Libretto."
                    "Britten's 'Prophetic Song': Tonal
                        Symbolism in *Billy Budd.*"
                    "Stage History and Critical
                        Reception."
    Donald Mitchell. "A *Billy Budd* Notebook
                    (1979-1991)."
    Philip Reed.   "From First Thoughts to First Night:
                        a *Billy Budd* Chronology."

49. Cooke, Mervyn.
    Britten and the Far East.
    Aldeburgh Studies in Music (pub. scheduled for 1996).

50. Corse, Sandra.
    Opera and the Uses of Language:
    Mozart, Verdi, and Britten.
    London: Associated University Presses, 1987. 163 p.
    ISBN 0-8386-3300-5. ML 1700 .C7.

    An interdisciplinary study of six operas—Mozart's
    Marriage of Figaro and *The Magic Flute,* Verdi's
    Otello and *Falstaff,* and Britten's *Owen Wingrave*
    and *Death in Venice.*

51. Crozier, Eric, ed.
    Benjamin Britten: Peter Grimes.
    London: John Lane, The Bodley Head, 1945. 55 p.
    (Sadler's Wells Opera Books, No. 3.)
    ML 410 .B84.

    This first collection of studies appeared at the time of the première of *Peter Grimes,* the composer's first operatic success, with Britten providing the often-quoted introduction as to motivation, rationale, and high hopes for a renaissance of English opera.

52. Crozier, Eric, ed.
    The Rape of Lucretia: A Symposium.
    London: John Lane, The Bodley Head, 1948. 101 p.
    MT 100 .B8.

    A richly illustrated commemorative volume which includes reproductions of the original designs for scenery and costumes by John Piper, photographs of the first productions at the Glyndbourne Opera House, and articles by Crozier, Henry Boys, John Piper, and Angus McBean. Britten's foreword gives insights into his views on the relationship between composer and librettist and the demands on both. Britten notes:

    > To be suitable for music, poetry must be simple, succinct and crystal clear; for many poets this must be a great effort, and the psychological epic poem to be read (or not read) in the quiet of the study is more attractive. I think they are wrong. Opera makes similar demands of conciseness on the composer. He must be able to paint a mood or an atmosphere in a single phrase and must search unceasingly for the apt one (p. 7).

---

53. Espina, Noni.
    Repertoire for the Solo Voice.
    Metuchen, N.J.: Scarecrow Press, 1977. 1290 p.
    ISBN 0-8108-0943-5. ML 128 .S3 E8.

An annotated guide to works for the solo voice published in modern editions and covering materials from the thirteenth century to the present. There is a substantial section on Britten The brief introduction, though updated in its chronological heading, hints at a need for final editing. Espina observes:

> Benjamin Britten, 1913-1976.
>
> Benjamin Britten, one of the most significant contemporary British composers, has done much to help elevate the role of the voice. . . His output of songs is growing . . .There is no doubt that much of his knowledge of writing for the voice was influenced by close association with the finest singers of his era. Much of his song writing comes in sets and cycles, several of which are introduced in this section. . . . Much more is still to be expected from . . . this truly outstanding English composer (p. 69).

Espina's annotated citations include:

> *A Charm of Lullabies; Seven Sonnets of Michelangelo; Les illuminations; On This Island; Our Hunting Fathers; Sechs Hölderlin-Fragmente; Songs and Proverbs of William Blake; The Holy Sonnets of John Donne; The Poet's Echo; Winter Words; The War Requiem;* and several solo songs.

---

54. Evans, Peter.
   The Music of Benjamin Britten.
   Rev. ed. London: J.M. Dent, 1989. 574 p.
   ISBN 0-460-12607-5. ML 410 .B853.

   First issued in 1979, this study of Britten's published works remains one of the most comprehensive examinations of his music. The analyses are discerning, scholarly, and stimulating, always encouraging the reader to return to the music. The book quickly became a 'classic' and is quoted by almost all subsequent contributors to Britten studies.

   The material is covered generically in 21 chapters, with a postscript added to the revised edition to include works published posthumously between 1979 and 1989. Most of the stage works, however, are treated individually in separate chapters. A bibliography and catalogue of works complete this valuable volume.

55. Howard, Patricia.
   The Operas of Benjamin Britten.
   New York: Frederick A. Praeger, 1969. 236 p.
   MT 100 B778 .H7.

   A well-written and perceptive introduction to each of Britten's operas (*Death in Venice* excepted, since it had not then been written), with a concluding chapter on "Britten and opera" which is cogent and concise.

56. Howard, Patricia, ed.
   The Turn of the Screw.
   Cambridge: Cambridge University Press, 1985. 164 p.
   ISBN 0-521-28356-6. ML 410 .B853 B47.

   One of a series of "Cambridge Opera Handbooks,"
   this critical study includes:

   John Evans.   "The (Music) Sketches:
                          Chronology and Analysis."
   Patricia Howard.   "Myfanwy Piper's *The Turn of
                          the Screw*: . . . Synopsis."
                       "(Music) . . . an Overall View."
                       "The Climax: Act II Scene 8, *Miles.*"
                       "*The Turn of the Screw* in the
                          Theatre."
   Vivien Jones.   "Henry James's *The Turn of the
                          Screw.*"
   Christopher Palmer.   "The Colour of the Music."

57. Herbert, David.
   The Operas of Benjamin Britten.
   New York: New Amsterdam Books, 1989. 384 p.
   ISBN 0-941533-71-9. ML 49 .B74 H5.

   Contains the full text of the libretti for each of
   Britten's 11 operas and five church parables, plus the
   text for the boys' vaudeville, *The Golden Vanity.* This
   illustrated volume includes a preface by Peter Pears
   and informative and entertaining essays by Janet
   Baker, Basil Coleman, Eric Crozier, Colin Graham,
   Hans Keller, John Piper, Myfanwy Piper, and Andrew
   Porter.

58. Jacobs, Arthur.
    Choral Music.
    London: Penguin Books, 1963. 444 p.
    ML 1500 .J3.

    "From the *Winchester Troper* (<u>ca</u>. A.D. 1000) to Benjamin Britten's *War Requiem* (1962)—such is the span of this symposium on music for human voices and it brings together more than twenty expert British and American contributors" (end page). Ernest Bradbury provides useful Britten entry (pp. 349-52).

59. Keller, Hans.
    Essays on Music.
    Christopher Wintle, ed.,
    with Bayan Northcott and Irene Samuel.
    Cambridge: Cambridge University Press, 1994. 269 p.
    ISBN 0-521-46216-9. ML 60 .K273.

    Thirty-nine essays, of which four are specially focused on Britten (the second, "Resistances to Britten's Music: Their Psychology" [1950]; the twenty-first, "*Gloriana* as Music Drama: a Reaffirmation" [1966]; the twenty-fifth, "Britten's Last Masterpiece" [1979]; and the thirty-seventh, "Why This Piece Is About *Billy Budd*" [1972]). Britten and his music serve as a point of reference or discussion for a number of other essays in this collection. Keller is an unabashed champion of Britten and uses his considerable analytical and discursive skill in the service of his cause. Regarded by many of his contemporaries as one of the most brilliant, as well as most provocative, of this century's musical scholars, Keller adds substantially to the analysis and understanding of Britten and his music.

60. May, Robin.
    Opera.
    London: Hodder and Stoughton, 1977. 216 p.
    ISBN 0-340-21847-9. ML 1700 .M19 O59.

    Includes a précis of Britten's contribution to the
    national and international operatic scene. In a concise
    summary of opera's status in Great Britain prior to
    Britten's arrival and of the consequences of his first
    considerable operatic success, May observes:

    > No excuse need be made for the amount of space
    > devoted here to *Grimes* because it is important to
    > stress its impact, which so ovewhelmed its first
    > audiences . . .In the modern British theatre only
    > the impact of John Osborne's *Look Back in
    > Anger* (1956) can be compared to it (pp. 175-
    > 176).

61. Mellers, Wilfrid.
    *Music in a New Found Land; Themes and
    Developments in the History of American Music.*
    New York: Knopf, 1965. 543 p.
    ML 200 .M44.

    In a comparison of Britten's style with that of Lukas
    Foss, Mellers writes:

    > If his [Foss's] virtuosity seems to lack a core
    > compared with that of Britten, we cannot
    > attribute that merely to the fact that Britten's
    > genius is the more deeper rooted in human
    > experience; there is also the fact that Britten had
    > an English tradition, and in particular Purcell, to
    > give direction to his eclecticism (p. 229).

62. Mellers, Wilfrid.
   Caliban Reborn: Renewal in Twentieth-century Music.
   London: Harper & Row, 1967, pp. 195.
   ML 197 .M265.

   Chapter VII includes a philosophical discussion of
   Britten's place in the scheme of twentieth-century
   music and a lengthy examination of Britten's church
   opera for children, *Noye's Fludde.*

63. Mitchell, Donald.
   Benjamin Britten: Paul Bunyan.
   London: Faber, 1988. 96 p.
   ISBN 0-571-15142-6. ML 50 .B8685 P3.

   W.H. Auden's libretto, with essay by Mitchell, "The
   Origins, Evolution and Metamorphoses of Paul Bunyan,
   Auden's and Britten's 'American' Opera."

64. Mitchell, Donald, ed.
   Benjamin Britten: Death in Venice.
   Cambridge University Press, 1987. 246 p.
   ISBN 0-521-31943-9. ML 410 .B853 B42.

   A collection of critical studies by an eminent roster of
   professionals and scholars, many of whom were
   involved with Britten in the creation and production of
   his last opera, thus providing an unusual sense of
   immediacy and intimacy in the writing. In an
   acknowledgement of the unique function of the
   archival resources at Aldeburgh, Mitchell notes:
   "Without virtually unrestricted access to the
   extraordinary documentary riches of the Britten-Pears
   Library and Archive at Aldeburgh, this book could
   certainly not be what it is."

Includes:

Patrick Carnegy. "The Novella Transformed: Thomas
                Mann as Opera."
Mervyn Cooke. "Britten and the Gamelan; Balinese
                Influences in *Death in Venice*."
John Evans.   "Twelve-Note Structures and
                Tonal Polarity."
Peter Evans.   "Synopsis: the Story, the Music not
                Excluded."
Colin Graham. "The First Production."
Colin Matthews.   "The *Venice* Sketchbook."
David Matthews. "*Death in Venice* and *the
                Third String Quartet.*"
Donald Mitchell. "An Introduction in the Shape of a
                Memoir."
Christopher Palmer. "Britten's *Venice* orchestra."
Myfanwy Piper. "The Libretto."
Philip Reed.   "Aschenbach Becomes Mahler:
                Thomas Mann as Film."
T.J. Reed.   "Mann and His Novella: *Death in
                Venice.*"
Ned Rorem.   "Britten's *Venice*."
Eric Roseberry. "Tonal Ambiguity in *Death in
                Venice*: a Symphonic View."
Rosamund Strode. "A *Death in Venice* Chronicle."
Wladyslaw Moes. "'I was Thomas Mann's Tadzio.'"
                (translated by Martin Cooper)

Includes four reviews of first performance (16.vi.73).
(a) Greenfield, Edward. *The Guardian,* 18.vi.73.
(b) Heyworth, Peter. *The Observer,* 24 vi.73.
(c) Northcott, Bayan. *The New Statesman,* 22.vi.73.
(d) Shaw-Taylor, D. *The Sunday Times,* 24.vi.73.

65. Routley, Eric.
    Twentieth Century Church Music.
    Rev. ed. London: Herbert Jenkins, 1966. 244 p.
    ML 3131 .R68.

An astute commentator on the state of church music in this century, Routley noted a decade before the composer's death that Britten's work represented a "watershed in English music." In a chapter titled "Letting in More Air," Routley observes that Britten's music up to 1940 is generally noteworthy for its brilliance and wit than for more profound qualities, but that with the composition of his *Sinfonia da requiem*, Britten had established himself as a composer to "be taken seriously." Routley states:

> It is then, from the point of view of the church, a piece of excellent fortune that so much of Britten's church music comes after 1940. . . . It is perhaps possible to come at the secret of Britten's remarkable success in church music if we consider him as making a third with two other composers we have especially paused on—Howells and Walton. . . . Britten is at a point equidistant from both: he neither consents to the traditional idiom as far as Howells does, nor dissents from it as obviously as Walton does. Moreover, while he has a touch, but only a touch, of the romantic, and a touch, but hardly more, of the Tudor in him, he is singular in having so great a love for Purcell. Nobody else reincarnates Purcell as Britten does (pp. 69-70).

66. Whittall, Arnold.
   The Music of Britten and Tippett:
   Studies in Themes and Techniques.
   2nd ed. Cambridge: Cambridge University Press, 1990.
   314 p.
   ISBN 0-521-38668-3. ML 390 .W38.

Whittall notes in his Prologue:

> Benjamin Britten and Michael Tippett have already been the subject of several separate studies, the number of which can confidently be expected to increase with some rapidity. For this reason alone, it might seem sound economic sense to compress two books into one. Nevertheless, my intention is to offer one book about two composers, rather than two books in one, since I believe that Britten and Tippett complement each other in striking and distinctive ways (p. 1).

In his treatment of Britten's oeuvre, Whittall's book may be viewed, in part, as both complementary and supplementary to the analyses and discourse of Peter Evans' major study *The Music of Benjamin Britten* (1989). The works selected for discussion are grouped under three principal heads, "The Thirties and the War," "After the War [1944-63]," and "Patterns of Transformation." Whittall wends his way through Britten's music in a manner that is both accessible and informative. While much of the information provided is not new, it is presented in quite an interesting form and the size of the volume makes it at once attractive.

Group 5

Various references

Aldeburgh and Glyndebourne
Histories and dictionaries
Miscellaneous

Aldeburgh and Glyndebourne

67. Blythe, Ronald.
   Aldeburgh Anthology.
   Aldeburgh: Snape Maltings Foundation in
   association with Faber Music, 1972. 457 p.
   ISBN 0-571-10005-1.

   Essays, reminiscences, pictures, and poetry based
   upon experiences of 25 Aldeburgh Festivals. Includes:

"A Festival in the Making."	"The Borough."
"In Memoriam E.M. Forster."	"Music in England."
"Aldeburgh Opera."	"North Sea Tide."
"Suffolk for the Naturalist."	"Thomas Hardy."
"Aldeburgh and Russia."	"Two Suffolk Poets."
"Children Singing."	"The Legacy."
"The Church Parables."	"Three Instruments."
"Ancient and Modern."	"Ancestors."
"Poems by William Blake."	"Profile."

   "'The Grey Disturbance' 1914-18, 1939-45."
   "Stravinsky's Tribute to Dylan Thomas."
   "Music in London, Venice, Vienna and Paris."

68. Brody, Elaine, and Claire Brook.
    The Music Guide to Great Britain.
    New York: Dodd, Mead, 1975. 240 p.
    ISBN 0-396-06955-X. ML 21 .B78.

    A "selective . . . reference tool and fact finder
    concerning the music life of England, Scotland,
    Wales, and Ireland," this volume contains information
    on the Aldeburgh Festival and its locality.

69. Burrows, Jill, comp.
    The Aldeburgh Story:
    A Pictorial History of the Aldeburgh Foundation.
    Aldeburgh: Aldeburgh Foundation, 1987. 68 p.

    Privately published for the Aldeburgh Foundation, this
    volume offers unique perspectives of the Aldeburgh
    Festival and Foundation, the successes, as well as the
    challenges, including the destruction of the first
    Maltings Concert Hall by fire in 1969 and its
    remarkably quick rebuilding in time for the next
    Aldeburgh Festival in 1970.

70. Higgins, John.
    Glyndebourne: A Celebration.
    London: Jonathan Cape, 1984. 172 p.
    ISBN 0-224-01905-8. ML 38 .G63 G642.

    Speaks of the strained relationship which had existed
    for many years between Glyndebourne and the
    Aldeburgh Festival and the happy prospect in 1985 of
    reconciling the two organizations and their operatic
    endeavors.

71. Hughes, Spike.
    Glyndebourne: A History of the Festival Opera.
    London: David & Charles, 1981. 388 p.
    ISBN 0-7153-7891-0. ML 38 .G63 G643.

    Comments on the cost of mounting the early Britten
    chamber operas *The Rape of Lucretia* and *Albert
    Herring* at Glyndebourne, as well as underwriting
    the overseas tours of the first two years of the
    English Opera Group.

72. Luckhurst, Nigel, photographer, John Amis,
    Richard Butt and Norman Scarfe, arrangers.
    A Photographer at The Aldeburgh Festival.
    Bury St. Edmunds: Alastair Press, 1990. 112 p.
    ISBN 1-870567-56-0. 780.7942646 (Dewey).

    Photographs taken by Luckhurst at five Aldeburgh
    Festivals (1974-78). Short essays introduce the
    photographer, the festival, and the location, along with
    commentary that is both witty and informative. John
    Amis' essay "Putting You In the Picture" speaks
    volumes concerning the somewhat remote location and
    small scale of the setting which cradled one of the
    most influential music festival series of the century.
    This essay also sketches the development of the
    festival and its supporting facilities. Amis writes:

    > Aldeburgh is a hundred miles from London on
    > the East Anglian coast facing what used to be
    > called the German Ocean, a small seaside place
    > north of Suffolk's county town, Ipswich, and
    > south of the port of Lowestoft where Benjamin
    > Britten was born . . .

For the first nineteen years the two chief venues of the Festival were the Parish Church and the Jubilee Hall in Aldeburgh, neither of them large. Even by the time the Hall had been rebuilt in 1960 it could still not hold more than 350 seats. Fortunately the 19th-century Malting-house in the nearby village of Snape (in sight of Britten's *Grimes* mill) became available; it was converted into an 850-seater multi-purpose concert-hall and open-stage auditorium. It was opened in time for the 1967 festival, burnt out on the opening night of the 1969 festival and rebuilt with astonishing speed to be ready for the 1970 session. From 1977 the Maltings also housed the Britten-Pears School for Advanced Studies. The acoustics of the Maltings are perfect, its interior plain but pleasing, its situation idyllic. Britten once remarked that it was the only concert hall in the world where you could walk out in the interval and see a red-shank.

In the pre-Maltings years Copland, Kodaly, Poulenc, Brain, and Ferrier took part; BB and PP performed countless times in each and every festival. . . . No other [festival] could boast such a roster of names and premières.

. . . A glance at the the list of music performed at the Festival up to the year 1987 reveals that, beside the two and a quarter pages devoted to the works of Britten, there are 74 pages devoted to the works of other composers, including well over a hundred premières (pp. 5-6).

73. Strode, Rosamund, comp.
*Music of Forty Festivals; A List of Works
Performed at Aldeburgh Festivals from 1948 to 1987.*
Aldeburgh: Britten Estate in association with
G. & I. Holst for the Aldeburgh Foundation and
the Britten-Pears Library, 1987. 79 p.
ISBN 0-9511939-1-0. 016.780780942646 (Dewey)

This useful compilation offers a survey of much of the
music performed at the first forty Aldeburgh Festivals
of Music and the Arts. In the words of the brief
introduction by Colin Matthews:

> The list provides a bird's-eye view of the
> thinking and planning of the Festival's artistic
> directors over the years. In this the major rôles
> were, of course, played in the past by Benjamin
> Britten and Peter Pears, together with Imogen
> Holst—whose contribution was particularly
> distinguished by her pioneering concerts of
> medieval music. The extraordinary diversity
> revealed speaks for itself, and as strongly in the
> music of the present century as elsewhere. The
> programmes were not restricted only to those
> composers towards whom the artistic directors
> were themselves sympathetic—indeed at the
> 1954 Festival (but not included here because
> the composers' names were not then recorded)
> was one of the first public performances in this
> country of *musique concrète,* something that
> was anathema to all three! (p. 2).

Histories and dictionaries

74. Abraham, Gerald.
100 Years of Music.
4th ed. London: Gerald Duckworth, 1974. 333 p.
ISBN 0-7156-07049. ML 196 .A3.

Abraham's view of Britten is representative of English criticism found two decades or more before the date of this edition: e.g.,

> The most successful English practitioner of yet another form of Gebrauchsmusik–music for radio plays and features–is Benjamin Britten, who possesses clever, facile technique and a remarkable gift for evoking mood or atmosphere with a very few notes; his music to Edward Sackville-West's The Rescue (1943) and Louis MacNeice's The Dark Tower (1946) should be models for radio and film composers (p. 293).

It may be noted here that terms such as "clever," and "facile technique," occur in early British journalistic comment on Britten and his music, sometimes reflecting suspicion of that rigorous professionalism, concerning the craft of composition, which Britten demonstrated and exemplified throughout his life.

75. Blom, Eric.
    Music In England.
    Rev. ed. London: Penguin Books, 1947, 288 p.
    Reprint; 1977. ML 285 .B6 M8.

    In this brief but brilliant treatment of the history and
    current state of music in his native country, English
    music critic Eric Blom wrote perceptively of one of
    the newest and brightest stars to appear in the national
    galaxy:

    > The youngest of those who can be said to be
    > established—the Benjamin in fact—is Britten.
    > As late as 1942, in the first edition of this book,
    > it was said that "his is a brilliantly versatile and
    > witty gift that only needs to be deepened by
    > experience to produce incontrovertible evidence
    > of exceptional genius. Meanwhile it is easy
    > enough to believe without evidence." Now, by
    > 1947, the evidence has arrived, and it is
    > incontrovertible (p. 269).

76. Blume, Friedrich, ed.
    *Die Musik in Geschichte und Gegenwart;
    allgemeine Enzyklopädie der Musik.*
    Kassel und Basel: Bärenreiter, 1952.
    Vol. 2, columns 323-327.
    ML 100 .M92.

    Written by Gerald Abraham, the article on Britten
    reflects judgments and views of the composer and his
    music prevalent among some English journalists in the
    late 1940s and early 1950s. The bibliography contains
    but one item—the first biography of Britten written by
    Eric Walter White.

77. Grout, Donald Jay, and Hermine Weigel Williams.
    A Short History of Opera.
    3rd ed. New York: Columbia University Press, 1988.
    913 p.
    ISBN 0-231-06192-7. ML 1700 .G83.

    Assessments of Britten in this latest edition of a
    standard text on opera reinforce the general estimate
    of Britten as an important twentieth-century operatic
    composer, e.g., from his Chapter 26, "The Recent
    Past":

    > All in all, there can be no question as to Britten's
    > signal importance in contemporary English opera
    > or his significance as an original, skillful, and
    > idealistic composer adapting himself without
    > sacrifice of integrity to the practical conditions of
    > his place and time (p. 544).

78. Howes, Frank Stewart.
    The English Musical Renaissance.
    New York: Stein and Day, 1966, pp. 381.
    ML 286 .H69.

    Assesses Britten's niche in the history of English
    music. "Since Purcell there has been no composer
    for the English stage of comparable stature. Single-
    handed he has transformed English operas"(p. 318).
    Refers also to Britten's religious music (pp. 306-
    307), and to his use of the anthology method as a
    source for cantata texts (p. 300).

79. Lebrecht, Norman.
   The Companion to 20th Century Music.
   New York: Simon & Schuster, 1992. 417 p.
   ISBN 0-671-66654-1. ML 100 .L46.

   Britten entry (pp. 50-54) is factual and interesting.

80. Rosenthal, Harold, and John Warrack.
   The Concise Oxford Dictionary of Opera.
   2nd ed. Oxford: Oxford University Press, 1979.
   reprinted with corrections, 1985. 561 p.
   ISBN 0-19-311321-X. ML 102 .06 R67.

   Offers commentary on Britten's contribution to the operatic repertoire and useful insights into the composer's national and personal roots.

81. Sadie, Stanley, ed.
   The New Grove Dictionary of Music and Musicians.
   London: Macmillan, 20 vols., 1980.
   ISBN 0-333-23111-2. ML 100 .N48.

   Peter Evans contributes a substantial article on Britten (vol. 3, pp. 293-308). Contrary to Evan's chronology, it was the Norwich Festival of October 30, 1927 (not 1924) at which Britten "attracted the interest of Frank Bridge, and became his pupil." Again, Britten was a piano student of Harold Samuel, but not at the Royal College of Music—having studied with Samuel prior to entering College where he was a pupil of Arthur Benjamin. (It is only fair to note that Evans corrects the first of these small inaccuracies in the second edition [1989] of his major study *The Music of Benjamin Britten.*)

81a. Sadie, Stanley, ed.
   History of Opera.
   New York: W.W. Norton, 1990.
   ISBN 0-393-02810-0. ML 1700 .H57.

   Contains a condensed version (pp. 302, 303-4, etc.) of
   Peter Evans' *New Grove* article on Britten.

82. Sadie, Stanley, ed.
   The New Grove Dictionary of Opera.
   London: Macmillan, 1992. 4 vols.
   ISBN 0-935859-92-6. ML 102 .O6N5.

   Arnold Whittall (vol. 1, pp. 606-9) provides a factual
   and perceptive introduction to Britten's operas,
   including a useful table of basic particulars
   concerning each work.

83. Slonimsky, Nicolas, ed.
   *The Concise Baker's Biographical
   Dictionary of Musicians.*
   New York: Schirmer Books, 1988. 1407 p.
   ISBN 0-02-872411-9. ML 105 .B16.

   An abridged version of the seventh edition of Baker's
   Biographical Dictionary of Musicians. The Britten
   entry (pp. 173-176) includes a brief biographical
   sketch (the age at which Britten began his regular
   studies with Frank Bridge was 14, not 13 as
   Slonimsky suggests) and a generous amount of space
   allotted to a catalog of the composer's music which
   records date of composition and date of first
   performance.

84. Trend, Michael.
The Music Makers: The English Musical
Renaissance from Elgar to Britten.
New York: Schirmer Books, 1985. 268 p.
ISBN 0-02-873090-9. ML Z86.4 .T74.

Offers a sweep through recent English musical
history, giving a context to Britten's achievement.
Like other writers, Trend couples Britten and Tippett.
"These two composers deserve to be treated together,
as did Elgar and Delius, as the outstanding figures of
English composition of their day" (p. 219). Includes:

"The English Musical Renaissance: A Nest of
Singing Birds."
"The English Environment: Elgar, Delius."
"Traditions—Old and New: Hurlstone,
Coleridge Taylor, Boughton, Holbrooke."
"Shifting Horizons: Bantock, Brian, Davies,
Smyth."
"Heirs and Rebels: Vaughan Williams, Holst,
Butterworth."
"Holding the Middle Ground: Bax, Ireland,
Bridge."
"The Frankfurt Gang: Gardiner, O'Neill,
Quilter, Scott, Grainger."
"The Shock of the New: Bliss, Walton,
Lambert, Berners, Warlock, Moeran."
"Traditions—New and Old: Gurney, Howells,
Bush, Rubbra, Finzi, Orr."
"Rebels and Heirs: Tippett, Britten."

85. Vaughan Williams, Ralph.

    National Music and Other Essays.

    2nd ed. Oxford: Oxford University Press, 1987. 312 p.
    ISBN 0-19-284016-9. ML 60 V288.

    Ralph Vaughan Williams' essays contain but one
    reference to Britten—sufficiently pertinent, however,
    to justify quotation here. Regardless of this, any
    student of Britten would do well to read all of
    Vaughan Williams on the subject of nationalism and
    music. Furthermore, it will be remembered that
    Vaughan Williams was one of three examiners (John
    Ireland and S.P. Waddington being the other two) to
    whom Britten presented himself for admission to the
    Royal College of Music, 9.vi.30, and who agreed to
    the awarding of a scholarship to the sixteen-year old
    student, despite some reservations by a member of the
    committee who was overheard remarking (perhaps it
    was S.P. Waddington) "What is an English public
    school boy doing writing music of this kind?"
    Vaughan Williams offers the following comment in
    his sixth essay, "A Minimum's Rest," dated 1948:

    > What was the life-giving power which led these
    > men [Parry, Stanford, and Elgar] to hand on the
    > torch of triumph? Time was when music by a
    > British composer meant rows of empty seats.
    > Now all is changed—why? Because all the
    > composers of this renaissance from Parry to
    > Britten, different and often antagonistic as their
    > aims often are, have this in common—that they
    > realize that vital art must grow in its own soil
    > and be nurtured by its own rain and sunshine
    > (p. 168).

86. Walker, Ernest.
   A History of Music in England.
   3rd ed. revised and enlarged by J.A. Westrup.
   Oxford: Clarendon Press, 1952. 468 p.
   ML 285 .W18.

   Reflects prevailing opinions of Britten and his music by a number of senior critics and scholars in the United Kingdom at that time.

87. White, Eric Walter.
   The Rise of English Opera.
   New York: Philosophical Library, 1951. 335 p.
   Facsimile reprint, New York: Da Capo, 1972.
   ISBN 0-306-71709-3. ML 1731 .W6.

Both the original edition (1951) and the facsimile reprint (1972) contain an introduction by Benjamin Britten. White's new foreword to the 1972 facsimile reprint is instructive in its self-evaluation and delineation of problems confronted in this pioneering study of English opera. For these reasons, and because of White's articulation of some issues of scholarship, excerpts from his foreword to the reprint are quoted here.

> This book arose out of a conviction that visitors to Great Britain during the Festival of Britain, 1951, would be interested to read an illustrated study of the new English operas that had appeared since the end of the Second World War—a comparatively modest project, but one that grew in size and scope as soon as I realized that such a study would have to be set in the context of the history of English opera.

At that point I discovered that serious histories of opera in general paid scant attention to English opera in particular, and that the authors of studies of British music usually betrayed signs of nervous insecurity when they found music being written for the theater instead of the church or concert hall. This meant that I had perforce to embark on a research campaign on my own, and with comparatively little time in which to carry it out. The final result was an improvement on my original plan, because at least it presented the important postwar renaissance of English opera in its proper perspective; but the book inevitably bears marks of haste with which it was written. To give only one example, it would be difficult to claim complete accuracy for the short list of English operas and semi-operas in Appendix A. Nevertheless, the greater part of the book is reasonably reliable, except for the entries for the final year (viz. 1951). These were based on advance information which was correct at the time of going to press; but in the event, dates and places of opera productions were changed, and in one case a title was altered at the last moment. As this reprint is a facsimile of the first edition, correcting these and other mistakes has not been possible; but those readers who wish at least to have a correct list of the English operas produced in 1951 are referred to my article, "A Decade of English Opera, 1951-1960," in *Theatre Notebook* 15-4 (1961) (pp. v-vi).

88. White, Eric Walter.
   A History of English Opera.
   London: Faber and Faber, 1983. 472 p.
   ISBN 0-571-10788-5. ML 1731 .W58.

   This is a major writing on English opera. It appeared
   as a sequel to White's earlier and more modest
   attempt to meet an evident need in this field (see
   citation III.87). White writes in his introduction:

   > The reader may legitimately ask—What are the
   > principles on which this history of English
   > opera has been written? . . .

   > I have thought of an English opera as being a
   > stage action with vocal and instrumental music
   > written by a British composer to a libretto in
   > English. This may include interludes, masques,
   > farce jigs, burlettas, as well as dramatic operas,
   > ballad operas, pasticcio operas, operettas, and
   > operas *tout court.*

   > This history deals with the composers of
   > English operas and their librettists, the
   > conditions in which their operas have been
   > produced on the stage, the public reaction
   > thereto, and the finances and administration
   > involved. Over a dozen composers are dealt
   > with in some depth—including Locke, Purcell,
   > Handel, Arne, Dibdin, Storace, Balfe, Sullivan,
   > Delius, Smyth, Boughton, Britten, and Tippett.

   White treats his material masterfully. His coverage of
   Britten's contribution to opera is comprehensive,
   sympathetic, and scholarly.

Miscellaneous

89. Auden, W.H., and Christopher Isherwood.
   Plays and other Dramatic Writings 1928-1938.
   Edward Mendelson, ed.
   Princeton: Princeton University Press, 1988. 680 p.
   ISBN 0-691-06740-6. PR 6001 .U4 A19.

90. Cooke, Deryck.
   The Language of Music.
   London: Oxford University Press, 1959. 289 p.
   ML 3845 .C68.

   Britten's *Albert Herring, Peter Grimes, Rape of Lucretia, Turn of the Screw,* and *The Holy Sonnets of John Donne* are quoted in this interesting exploration of music's linguistic functions. The study offers a commentary on aspects of Britten's particular use of tonal conventions for dramatic and expressive effect.

91. Marco, Guy.
   Opera: A Research and Information Guide.
   New York: Garland Publishing, 1984. 373 p.
   ISBN 0-8240-8999-5. ML 128.04 M28.

   Primarily an annotated bibliography, this concise *Guide* offers assistance to a broad spectrum of readership—from "scholars involved in research" to "anyone—specialist or layman—who simply wants a fact or two about opera" (p. xv). While specific reference to Britten is brief (seven citations [226-232] with incisive and insightful annotation), the sweep of this bibliographic overview of operatic source material makes it a desirable reference tool for background studies on Britten and opera.

Group 6

University studies

Topical index
Baccalaureate theses
Master's theses
Doctoral dissertations

This group of entries provides an overview, spanning more than four decades, of college and university theses and dissertations which focus, either broadly or narrowly, on some aspect of Benjamin Britten and his music. One hundred and seventy-five titles are cited here, 19 of which are baccalaureate theses (mostly British or European), 77 are master's theses, and 79 are doctoral dissertations. While many of these studies, especially those completed in partial fulfillment of advanced degree requirements, are scholarly and mostly useful documents, few have found commercial publishers and their circulation remains limited. The inclusion of these titles here, however, hints at the range of interest in Britten studies and the possibilities of further research, as well as facilitating access to information on and about Britten not otherwise available in published form.

Topical index

The topical index to university studies includes the following, broadly defined categories, some of which are subdivided to facilitate research. Citations are referenced to entry numbers.

People and places
Influences
Instrumental studies
Choral studies
Church music studies
Operatic studies
Vocal studies
Style studies
Incidental music studies
Studies of specific compositions.

PEOPLE and PLACES

Aldeburgh Festival
Rowsell, 103

Auden, W.H.
Burgess, 117
Jennings, 229

Britten, Benjamin
Elliott, 212
Gabbard, 218

**Britten-Pears Library
and other libraries**
Rudnick, 171
Thacker, 183

INFLUENCES

Bali
Cooke, 121
Moon, 244

China
Hsu, 226

England
Bolte, 92
Kovnatskaya, 230

Japan
Rhoads, 250

Oriental
Cooke, 204
Ketukaenchan, 143

INSTRUMENTAL STUDIES

Cello
Baker, 192
Clark, 203
Cooke, 120
Holloway, 135
Low, 234
Taggart, 259
Tiemeyer, 261

Guitar
Dwyer, 124
Mosley, 155

Harp
Kemp, 142

Horn
Chenoweth, 202

Percussion
Sanderson, 172

Piano
Hanson, 223

String quartet
Martel, 152
Millard, 101
Rupprecht, 104

CHORAL STUDIES

Boos, 198
Bryce, 115
Damp, 205
Dundore, 211
Goetz, 220
Hansler, 222
Hart, 224
Hurstad, 227
Kirby, 145
MacPherson, 236
Schiavone, 174

CHURCH MUSIC STUDIES

Bennett, 194
Goetz, 220
Hurstad, 227
Kirby, 145
Page, 161
Powell, 164
Rauch, 168
Turner, 108

OPERATIC STUDIES

Rambo, 166
Robison, 251
Scott, 176
Simons, 254
Smedley, 255
Snyder, 256

VOCAL STUDIES

Berlin, 196
Brewster, 201
Hladky, 133
Houghland, 136
Lewin, 149
Litten, 233
Ramirez, 167
Stilgebaurer, 182
Tibbets, 260
Upton, 186
Whitmire, 265
Wilson, 110

STYLE STUDIES

Delmore, 208
Jenkins, 228
Kyle, 147
Lewin, 149
Mark, 237
Pouncy, 163
Reiser, 169
Rupprecht, 252
Scherr, 173
Scott, P., 105
Scott, R., 176
Stallings, 257
Stroeher, 258
Whitesell, 264
Young, 187

Baccalaureate theses

92. Bolte, John C. BA, Drew University, 1972.
"Benjamin Britten, Michael Tippett and
the English Musical Renaissance."

93. Cambell, Fiona. BM, U. of Newcastle Upon Tyne, 1990.
"*Owen Wingrave:* Stage or Screen?
a Study of Benjamin Britten's Opera."

94. Cooke, Mervyn J. BA, University of Cambridge, 1984.
"Dramatic and Musical Cohesion in Britten's
A Midsummer Night's Dream."

95. Cushing, Gloria. BM, St. Olaf College, 1972.
"Benjamin Britten's *A Charm of Lullabies.*"

96. Diana, Barbara. BM, Università Degli Studi di Pavia,
1993. "Il sapore della conoscenza: Benjamin Britten e
Death in Venice."

97. Henderson, Judith. BA, University of Cambridge, 1991.
"Structural Tonality in Britten's
The Burning Fiery Furnace."

98. Keohane, S. BM, University of Manchester, 1971.
"The Operas of Benjamin Britten from
Peter Grimes to *Gloriana.*"

99. Kilmister, Penny. BM, University of Birmingham, 1983.
"*Death in Venice:* Britten's Transformation
of the Novella by Thomas Mann."

100. Maria, Isabella. BA, Università Degli Studi di Torino,
        1990. "L'opera da camera di Britten:
            The Turn of the Screw nel contesto europeo."

101. Millard, James. BA, University of Durham, 1990.
        "An Analysis of Formal and Thematic
            Structure in Britten's String Quartets."

102. Newill, Heather. BM, University of Sheffield, 1978.
        "Paul Bunyan: Critical Study of an Operetta
            by W.H. Auden and Benjamin Britten."

103. Rowsell, Janet. BA, Bath Polytechnic, 1979.
        "A Composer in a Community:
            Britten and the Aldeburgh Festival from 1948-1968:
            His Response as a Composer to the Limitations and
            Advantages of His Immediate Environment."

104. Rupprecht, Philip. BA, University of Cambridge, 1988.
        "The Harmonic Language of
            Britten's *String Quartet No. 3."*

105. Scott, Phillip. BA, University of Sydney, 1974.
        "Britten's Use of the Passacaglia."

106. Sinden-Evans, Rosie. BMus, University of London, 1993.
        "In Peace I Have Found My Image:
            Britten and the Pacificst Ideal
            with Particular Reference to *Owen Wingrave."*

107. Toogood, Catherine. BEd, Rolle College, Exmouth, 1983.
        "An Introductory Study of Benjamin Bitten's
            Children's Operas: *Let's Make an Opera,*
            and *Noye's Fludde."*

108. Turner, Stephanie. BM, Butler University, 1972.
     "Representative Works of
         Benjamin Britten's Church Music."

109. Watson, Gary. BM, University of Sydney, 1985.
     "Curlew River as Holy Theatre."

110. Wilson, Robert G. BM, University of Aberdeen, 1982.
     "Elements of Textual and Musical Structure
         and Interpretation in the Song Cycles of
         Benjamin Britten."

Master's theses

111. Allen, Debra K. MM, North Texas State University, 1982.
     "Drama and Characterization in Opera Settings of
         A Midsummer Night's Dream
         by Britten and Siegmeister."

112. Arthur, William N. MA,
         Arizona State College, Flagstaff, 1963.
     "A Stylistic Analysis of Four Choral Compositions
         in Four Periods of Music History:
         The Seasons, Joseph Haydn,
         Requiem, Gabriel Fauré,
         A Ceremony of Carols, Benjamin Britten,
         Christ lag in Todesbanden, J.S. Bach."

113. Bauer, Julia. MM,
        Ludwig-Maximilians-Universität Munich, 1992.
        "Purcell—Bearbeitungen Brittens am Beispiel
        von *Orpheus Britannicus—Seven Songs.*"

114. Brashear, Ann. MM, Northern Illinois University, 1986.
        "*Winter Words, Op. 52,* by Benjamin Britten:
        an Analysis."

115. Bryce, Michael. MM,
        SW Baptist-Theological Seminary, 1982.
        "A Conductor's Analysis of Selected Works by
            Andrea Gabrieli, Jacob Handl, W.A. Mozart
            Anton Bruckner, Benjamin Britten,
            Daniel Pinkham, and Vincent Persichetti."

116. Buccheri, John S. MA, Eastman School of Music, 1965.
        "Aspects of Form, Melody, and Harmony in
            the *War Requiem* by Benjamin Britten."

117. Burgess, Sharon. MA, Ball State University, 1980.
        "A Study of Benjamin Britten's and W.H. Auden's
            Collaborative Compositions, 1932-1939."

118. Chance, Von Darnell. MA, University of Tennessee, 1978.
        "The Use of Borrowed Musical Materials in
            Benjamin Britten's *War Requiem* and
            Igor Stravinsky's *Requiem Canticles.*"

119. Chiles, Harvey M. MM, Bowling Green State U., 1980.
        "An Analysis of Benjamin Britten's
            Rejoice in the Lamb."

120. Cooke, Mervyn J. MPh, University of Cambridge, 1985.
"An Analysis of the Second Movement (Scherzo) from
Symphony for Cello and Orchestra Op. 68."

121. Cooke, Mervyn J. MPh, University of Cambridge, 1985.
"Britten and Bali; a Study in Stylistic Synthesis."

122. Coolidge, Sandra A. MA, Texas Woman's U., 1970.
"A Director's Study and Prompt Book of
The Turn of the Screw by Benjamin Britten."

123. Davis, Charles R. MM,
SW Baptist-Theological Seminary, 1971.
"A Conductor's Analysis of
Laudes organi and Te Deum by Zoltan Kodaly,
Cantata misericordium by Benjamin Britten."

124. Dwyer, Benjamin. MM, University of London, 1992.
"The Guitar Works of Benjamin Britten."

125. Elam, Charlotte M. MM, East Texas State U., 1978.
"*Charm of Lullabies:* Text and Musical Style."

126. Fancher, Joseph E. MA, San Francisco State U., 1989.
"A Musico-dramatic Analysis of
A Boy Was Born, Op. 3 of Benjamin Britten."

127. Foster, Michael S. MA, New Mexico Highlands U., 1982.
"A Biographical Delineation of Edward Benjamin
Britten and an Analytical Synopsis of His
Serenade, for Tenor, Horn, and Strings, Op. 31."

128. Frackenpohl, David J. MM, North Texas State U., 1986.
"Analysis of *Nocturnal, Op. 70,* by Benjamin Britten."

129. Ginn, Michael. MPh, University of Oxford, 1992.
     "Benjamin Britten's *Peter Grimes*
        and *The Turn of the Screw:*
        a Study of Opera Libretti."

130. Gowers, Jean M. MM, University of Surrey, 1983.
     " *'What Has She Written?'* " (*The Turn of the Screw*).

131. Greco, Antonia M. MA, Hofstra University, 1976.
     "Musical Symbolism and the Functional Use of
        the Orchestra in Benjamin Britten's
        The Rape of Lucretia. "

132. Greuling, Corinne M. MA, U. of Connecticut, 1978.
     "A Stylistic Analysis of Benjamin Britten's
        A Ceremony of Carols for Purposes of
        Interpretation and Choral Performance Practice."

133. Hladky, Keyte M. MA, University of Oregon, 1986.
     "Benjamin Britten's Settings of English Sonnets."

134. Hodgins, J. MA, University of British Columbia, 1981.
     "Orientalism in Benjamin Britten's *Curlew River.* "

135. Holloway, Sarah. MM, University of Texas-Austin, 1982.
     "Benjamin Britten, *Suite for Cello, Op. 72:*
        a Commentary."

136. Houghland, Lynda G. MA, U. of North Carolina, 1969.
     "Unity in the Solo Song Cycles of Benjamin Britten."

137. Hwang, Der Shin. MFA, U. of Cal., Los Angeles, 1988.
     "Performance Practice Problems in
        Benjamin Britten's Song Cycle
        A Charm of Lullabies, Op. 41."

138. Jacobson, A.S. MMus, University of London, 1980.
     "Analysis of *Journey of the Magi* (Canticle IV)."

139. Johnson, Jennifer. MA, Louisiana State U., 1987.
     "The Metadramatic Dimensions of Benjamin Britten's
        A Midsummer Night's Dream."

140. Jonson, Joanne M. MA, University of Minnesota, 1959.
     "A Production Thesis of
        Benjamin Britten's *Let's Make an Opera.*"

141. Kelly, Diane R. MA, West Carolina University, 1986.
     "*Tit for Tat* by Benjamin Britten:
        a Lecture Recital."

142. Kemp, Julie. MM, Bowling Green State University, 1987.
     "Benjamin Britten's *Suite for Harp Op. 83:*
        an Interpretative Essay for Performance."

143. Ketukaenchan, Sonsak. MA, University of York, 1984.
     "The Oriental Influence on Benjamin Britten."

144. Kiger, James E. MA, Indiana State University, 1972.
     "A Comprehensive Melodic Analysis of
        Curlew River: Church Parable by Benjamin Britten."

145. Kirby, Claude O. MM.
      SW Baptist-Theological Seminary, 1980.
      "A Conductor's Analysis of Selected Choral Works
         by Orlandus Lassus, Claudio Monteverdi,
         Heinrich Schulz, Benjamin Britten,
         and Jean Berger."

146. Kishinami, Yukiko. MM, University of London, 1990.
      "The Operatic Treatment of Supernatural Characters
         in Britten's *A Midsummer Night's Dream*."

147. Kyle, James D. MM.
      SW Baptist-Theological Seminary, 1961.
      "The Recitative in the Dramatic Vocal Works of
         Benjamin Britten."

148. Leavens, Kenneth S. MA, Cal. State U, Fullerton, 1976.
      "The Preparation and Performance of Britten's
         Missa brevis in D, Op. 63
         for Boys' Voices and Organ."

149. Lewin, Ann R. MA, U. of Cal., Los Angeles, 1964.
      "Text Setting in the Songs of Benjamin Britten."

150. Maddox, Donald. MM,
      SW Baptist-Theological Seminary, 1970.
      "Benjamin Britten: a Conductor's Analysis of
         Saint Nicolas."

151. Malloy, Antonia. MA, University of Surrey, 1990.
      "*Owen Wingrave:* a 'Libretto-eyed View.' "

152. Martel, Robert N. MA, University of Connecticut, 1987.
"Benjamin Britten's *String Quartet No. 2 in C, Op. 36*
Analytical Observations on the *Chacony.*"

153. Martin, Phillip R. MM,
SW Baptist-Theological Seminary, 1969.
"An Analysis of Benjamin Britten's *Noye's Fludde.*"

154. McNeff, Paul. MA, California State U., Fullerton, 1980.
"Vocal Registers: a Functional Analysis Relating to the
Singing Performance of Selected Songs from *The
Holy Sonnets of John Donne* by Benjamin Britten."

155. Mosley, Michael. MM, Indiana University, 1969.
"Twentieth-century Guitar Idiom as Reflected
in Compositions by Berkeley, Britten, and Martin."

156. Nelson, David. MM, Hardin-Simmons University, 1987.
"Benjamin Britten's *Rejoice in the Lamb;*
Historical Perspectives and Performance Practices."

157. Nickels, Samuel V. MM, Florida State University, 1985
"The Influence of Text and Harmony on the
Formation of Melody in Benjamin Britten's
Rejoice in the Lamb."

158. Nicolai, Annette. MM, Cal. State U., Long Beach, 1992.
"Benjamin Britten's *A Charm of Lullabies;*
Historical Survey, Analysis, and Performance."

159. Nitschke, Brad. MM, Bowling Green State U., 1985.
"Benjamin Britten's *A Ceremony of Carols:*
a Study and Analysis."

160. Novak, Elizabeth G.M. MS, Louisiana State U., 1982.
     "*A Ceremony of Carols:*
         a Program of Liturgical Dance."

161. Page, Gordon K. MM,
         SW Baptist-Theological Seminary, 1978.
         "The Leitmotif in the Parables for Church
         Performance by Benjamin Britten."

162. Pooler, Marie. MM, Cal. State U., Fullerton, 1971.
         "Analysis of Choral Settings of the *Te Deum*
         by the Contemporary Composers Benjamin Britten,
         Leo Sowerby, Halsey Stephens,
         and Vincent Persichetti."

163. Pouncy, Sian L. MA, University of Wales, 1975.
         "The Variation Concept in the Works
         of Benjamin Britten."

164. Powell, John. MA, University of Cambridge, 1973.
         "Britten's Church Parables, with Particular Reference
         to Their Japanese Origins."

165. Preble, Deborah J. MA, Cal. State U., Fullerton, 1980.
         "Benjamin Britten's *Rejoice in the Lamb*."

166. Rambo, Carol Sue Piskac. MM, U. of Nebraska, 1974.
         "Benjamin Britten: Three Representative Operas."

167. Ramirez, Marshall. MA, Cal. State U., Long Beach, 1979.
         "Word Painting and Textual Treatment
         in Selected Songs of Benjamin Britten."

168. Rauch, Marcella. MA, Ouachita Baptist U., 1969.
    "Benjamin Britten's Contribution to Church Music."

169. Reiser, David A. MA, University of North Dakota, 1965.
    "The Solo Vocal Music of Benjamin Britten:
    the Effect of the Text upon the Music."

170. Rogers, Jerome S. MM, S. Illinois U., Carbondale, 1977.
    "A Study of the Relationship between Poetry
    and Music in Benjamin Britten's Song Cycle
    Who are these children? Op. 84."

171. Rudnick, Tracey. MM, University of Texas, Austin, 1992.
    "Britten-related holdings in The Harry Ransom
    Humanities Research Center;
    an Annotated Catalog."
    (See citation III.9.)

172. Sanderson, Gillian. MM, University of Alberta, 1980.
    "The Dramatic Role of Percussion in
    Selected Operas of Benjamin Britten."

173. Scherr, Suzanne C. MA, California-Los Angeles, 1981.
    "Non-determined Temporal Devices in Post-1960
    Britten; an Analytical Investigation."

174. Schiavone, Suzanne C. MA, U. College of Wales, 1981.
    "Aspects of Style in Britten's Choral Music;
    with Particular Reference to Word-setting
    and to the Practical Aspects of His Composition."

175. Scholl-Pederson, K. MA, U.of Copenhagen, 1976.
     "Benjamin Britten; *The Turn of the Screw:* an
         Exemplification of Britten's Operatic Ideas."

176. Scott, Richard O. MA, Eastern Illinois University, 1967.
     "Two Operas of Benjamin Britten:
         an Analysis of Style."

177. Shuffield, Joseph Nelson. MM, Baylor University, 1995.
     "Nattiez's Tripartition as an Analytical Strategy for
         Britten's *The Turn of the Screw.*"

178. Siemens, Stephanie L. MFA, U. of Texas, Austin, 1984.
     "A Production Thesis on *Albert Herring.*"

179. Skelley, Barbara J. MM, Bowling Green State U., 1976.
     "'Before Life and After' from *Winter Words:*
         a Song Cycle for High Voice and Piano
         by Benjamin Britten."

180. Smith, Lisa. MM, University of London, 1992.
     "Britten's *Piano Concerto*:
         Sources and Performance Issues."

181. Smith, Sara E. MA, Eastman School of Music, 1983.
     "A Study and Analysis of the Instrumental Theme
         and Variations in Benjamin Britten's
         The Turn of the Screw."

182. Stilgebaurer, Marilyn K. MS, Eastern Illinois U., 1961.
     "An Analysis of the Vocal Problems
         of Selected Works by Benjamin Britten."

183. Thacker, Martin. MPh, Polytechnic, North London, 1986.
"The Organisation of Composer Archives; with Special
Reference to The Britten-Pears Library, Aldeburgh."
(See citation III.10.)

184. Thomas, Catriona. MM,
Ludwig-Maximilian Universität, München, 1985.
"Untersuchungen zu Britten's *War Requiem*, Op. 66."

185. Turner, Robert F. MA, Claremont College, 1958.
"An Examination of Benjamin Britten's
Serenade for Tenor, Horn, and Strings."

186. Upton, Leone S. MA, Tulane University, 1968.
"The Solo Song Cycles of Benjamin Britten
with Piano Accompaniment, through 1965."

187. Young, Jack. MM, Baylor University, 1986.
"World War II and its Effects on Selected English,
French, and Russian Composers."
(Benjamin Britten, Olivier Messiaen,
and Dimitri Shostakovitch.)

Doctoral dissertations

188. Arfsten, Glen D. DMA, University of Alabama, 1990.
"An Analytical Study for the Performance of
Canticle V: The Death of Saint Narcissus."

189. Aslanian, Vahbe. DMA, Stanford University, 1962.
"*Cantata academica: Carmen basiliense.*"

190. Bach, Jan. DMA, University of Illinois, 1971.
   "An Analysis of Britten's
      A Midsummer Night's Dream."

191. Bagley, Peter Belvy Eugene. DM, Indiana U., 1972.
   "Britten's *War Requiem:* a Structural Analysis."

192. Baker, Charles A.. DMA, Eastman School of Music, 1965.
   "An Analytical Study of the *Sonata in C for Cello and
      Piano* by Benjamin Britten."

193. Barker, Jon Albert. DMA, Louisiana State U., 1977.
   "A Musical Analysis of
      Songs and Proverbs of William Blake, Op. 74
      by Edward Benjamin Britten."

194. Bennett, Glenn M. DMA,
      SW Baptist-Theological Seminary, 1988.
   "A Performer's Analysis and Discussion of
      the Five Canticles of Benjamin Britten."

195. Benser, Jerry Ray. DMA, University of Iowa, 1990.
   "A Singer's Commentary on the
      Winter Words of Benjamin Britten."

196. Berlin, Myrna Genevieve. DMA, University of Iowa, 1986.
   "Vowel Intelligibility Problems in
      Selected Solo Vocal Works of Benjamin Britten."

197. Bernard, Andrew. DMA, University of Washington, 1990.
   "Two Musical Perspectives of Twentieth-century
      Pacificism; an Analytical and Historical View of
      Britten's *War Requiem* and Bernstein's *Kaddish
      Symphony.*"

198. Boos, Kenneth G. DMA, University of Miami, 1986.
"A Study of the Relationship between Text
and Music in Five Selected Choral Works
of Benjamin Britten."

199. Boubel, Karen A. PhD, U. of Wisconsin, Madison, 1985.
"The Conflict of Good and Evil; a Musical and
Dramatic Study of Britten's *Billy Budd*."

200. Brace, Patricia Lynne. PhD, Ohio University, 1993.
"A Rhetorical Study of Coventry Cathedral and
Benjamin Britten's *War Requiem* Revealing
the Tropes of Metonymy, Metaphor and Irony."

201. Brewster, Robert G. PhD, Washington University, 1967.
"The Relationship between Poetry and Music
in the Original Solo-Vocal Works of
Benjamin Britten through 1965."

202. Chenoweth, Richard K. DMA, U. of Cincinnati, 1988.
"The Horn in Opera; a Study in Orchestration
With a Focus on Selected Operas by Britten
and Strauss."

203. Clark, Anne Louise. DMA, U. of Texas, Austin, 1988.
"Innovative Writing for the Cello in the
Three Suites of Benjamin Britten."

204. Cooke, Mervyn J. PhD, University of Cambridge, 1988.
"Oriental Influences in the Music of Benjamin Britten."

205. Damp, Alice B. DMA, Eastman School of Music, 1973.
"The Fusion of Sacred and Secular Elements
in Benjamin Britten's Vocal and Choral Literature."

206. Dauer, Robin Lee. DMA, University of Cincinnati, 1994.
"Three Works for Voice and French Horn with
Accompaniment (J.S. Bach: 'Quoniam tu solus
sanctus' from *B Minor Mass*; Franz Schubert:
'Auf dem strom;' Benjamin Britten: *Serenade,*
Op. 31, for Tenor, Horn, and Strings)."

207. Deavel, R. Gary. PhD, Eastman School of Music, 1970.
"A Study of Two Operas by Benjamin Britten:
Peter Grimes and *Turn of the Screw.*"

208. Delmore, John Patrick. DMA, U. of Arizona, 1991.
"Benjamin Britten's Canticles and Their Literary,
Thematic, and Musical Unity with his Operas."

209. Desblache, Lucile.
Université de Paris VIII Saint Denis, 1987.
"Autour d'*Albert Herring;* recherches sur
l'expression de l'humor dans la musique vocale
et lyrique de Benjamin Britten."

210. Douglas, Earl B. DMA, U. of Texas, Austin, 1987.
"A History and Analysis of Benjamin Britten's
Who Are These Children? Op. 84."

211. Dundore, Mary Margaret. DMA, U. of Washington, 1969.
"The Choral Music of Benjamin Britten."

212. Elliott, Graham John. PhD, U. of Wales, Bangor ,1985.
"Benjamin Britten: the Things Spiritual."
(See citation III.16.)

213. Emmons, Celeste Mildred. DMA, University of
   North Carolina at Greensboro, 1994.
   "*Our Hunting Fathers* by Benjamin Britten and
   W.H. Auden: A Musical and Textual Analysis."

214. England, Gordon A. EdD, U. of Northern Colorado, 1972.
   "A Study to Provide Self-administering Improvement
   in Conducting Specific Rhythmic Problems
   in Two Choral Works of Benjamin Britten:
   Rejoice in the Lamb and *Te Deum*."

215. Evans, John. PhD, University of Wales, Cardiff, 1984.
   "Benjamin Britten's *Death in Venice*;
   Perspectives on an Opera."

216. Feldman, James. PhD, Kent State University, 1987.
   "The Musical Portrayal of Gustav von Aschenbach
   in Benjamin Britten's *Death in Venice*."

217. Fougerousse, James. PhD,
   Leopold-Franzens, Innsbruck 1975.
   "*Billy Budd;* from Novel to Opera."

218. Gabbard, James H. EdD, Cal. State U., Fullerton, 1969.
   "Benjamin Britten; His Music, the Man, and His Time."

219. Godsalve, William H. L. PhD, U. of Saskatchewan, 1990.
   "Opera from Comedy: Britten Remakes
   Shakespeare's 'Dream.' "

220. Goetz, Thomas Eldon. DMA, Northwestern U., 1990.
   "Britten's Church Music: the Short Choral Works
   and *AMDG*."

221. Hall, William D. DMA, U. of Southern California, 1970.
"The Requiem Mass; a Study of Performance Practices
from the Baroque Era to the Present Day as Related
to Four Requiem Settings by Gilles, Mozart, Verdi,
and Britten."

222. Hansler, George E. PhD, New York University, 1957.
"Stylistic Characteristics and Trends in the Choral
Music of Five Twentieth-century British Composers;
a Study of the Choral Work of Benjamin Britten,
Gerald Finzi, Constant Lambert, Michael Tippett,
William Walton."

223. Hanson, J.R. PhD, Eastman School of Music, 1969.
"Macroform in Selected Twentieth Century
Piano Concertos."

224. Hart, Ralph Eugene. PhD, Northwestern University, 1952.
"Compositional Techniques in Choral Works of
Stravinsky, Hindemith, Honegger, and Britten."

225. Herbert, Rembert Bryce. PhD, American U., D.C., 1974.
"An Analysis of *Nine Holy Sonnets of John Donne:*
Set to Music by Benjamin Britten."

226. Hsu, Ti-Fei. DMA, American Cons. of Music, 1988.
"Chinese Influence in Four Twentieth-century Song
Cycles by Roussel, Carpenter, Griffes, Britten."

227. Hurstad, Linda. DMA, University of Texas, Austin, 1987.
"Benjamin Britten's Sacred Works for Voices and
Organ; an Analysis with Performance Suggestions
for Choral Conductors."

228. Jenkins, Susan Elaine. DMA, Ohio State University, 1984.
     "Representationalism in Selected Twentieth-century
          Compositions About the Sea (Claude Debussy,
          George Crumb, Benjamin Britten)."

229. Jennings, John W. DMA, University of Illinois, 1979.
     "The Influence of W.H. Auden on Benjamin Britten."

230. Kovnatskaya, Ludmila. DA, Leningrad State U., 1987.
     "Bendzhamin Britten i angliiskaya muzyka
          nervoi poloviny XX veka."

231. Lewis, Gail Diane. DMA, U./Wisconsin, Madison, 1995.
     "Benjamin Britten's Writing for Horn with Tenor
          Voice: *Serenade, Op. 31*; 'The Heart of the Matter,'
          Nocturne, Op. 60."

232. Lickey, Eugene Harold. DM, Indiana University, 1969.
     "An Analysis of Benjamin Britten's *Serenade, Op. 31.*"

233. Litten, Jack Dane. EdD, Columbia University, 1969.
     "Three Song Cycles of Benjamin Britten."

234. Low, D.G. DM, Northwestern University, 1973.
     "The Solo Cello Music of Felix Mendelssohn;
          the Cello Sonatas of Boni, Scipriani, and Vandini;
          Solo Cello Chamber Music of Benjamin Britten."

235. Lundergan, Edward. PhD, U. of Texas, Austin, 1991.
     "Benjamin Britten's *War Requiem:*
          Stylistic and Technical Sources."

236. MacPherson, Scott A. DMA, U. of Southern Cal., 1992.
     "The Posthumously Published Choral Works
        of Benjamin Britten."

237. Mark, Christopher Michael. PhD, Southampton, 1989.
     "Stylistic and Technical Evolution
        in the Early Music of Britten."

238. Marsh, M. PhD, London, 1983.
     "Turn of the Screw; Britten's and Piper's
        Operatic Fulfillment of Henry James's Novella."

239. Mayer, Mark. EdD, Columbia University, 1983.
     "A Structural and Stylistic Analysis of the Benjamin
        Britten *Curlew River.*"

240. McGiffert, Genevieve. PhD, University of Denver, 1970.
     "The Musico-dramatic Techniques of
        Benjamin Britten: Detailed Study of *Peter Grimes.*"

241. Meister, Barbara. PhD, City U. of New York, 1987.
     "The Interaction of Music and Poetry: a Study of
        Paul Verlaine as Set to Music by Claude Debussy
        and of the Song Cycle *Songs and Proverbs of
        William Blake* by Benjamin Britten."

242. Mertz, Margaret Stover. PhD, Harvard University, 1990.
     "History, Criticism and the Sources of
        Benjamin Britten's *Rape of Lucretia.*"

243. Milliman, Joan Ann. PhD, U. of Southern Cal., 1977.
     "Benjamin Britten's Symbolic Treatment of Sleep,
        Dream, and Death as Manifest in His Opera
        Death in Venice."

244. Moon, Kyung Soo. DMA, U. of Texas, Austin, 1993.
"Balinese Influences in Benjamin Britten's
Songs from the Chinese, Op. 58."

245. Oosting, Stephen. DMA, Eastman School of Music, 1985.
"Text-music Relationships in Benjamin Britten's
Serenade for Tenor, Horn and Strings."

246. Packales, Joseph. PhD, Kent State University, 1984.
"Benjamin Britten's *Peter Grimes;* an Analysis."

247. Page, Gordon Keith. DMA,
SW Baptist-Theological Seminary, 1991.
"Melodic Unification in
Benjamin Britten's *War Requiem.*"

248. Phillips, Betty Lou. DMA, U. of Texas, Austin, 1989.
"Relationships Between Text and Music in
Benjamin Britten's Song Cycle *Les illuminations.*"

249. Reed, Philip. PhD, University of East Anglia, 1987.
"The Incidental Music of Benjamin Britten;
a Study and Catalogue of His Music for
Film, Theatre, and Radio."
(See citation III.8.)

250. Rhoads, Mary Ruth S. PhD, Michigan State U., 1969.
"Influences of Japanese 'Hogaku' Manifest in
Selected Compositions by Peter Mennin and
Benjamin Britten."

251. Robison, Clayne Wilcox. DMA, U. of Washington, 1973.
"Documentation of Two Opera Productions;
Slow Dusk by Carlisle Floyd and
Noye's Fludde by Benjamin Britten."

252. Rupprecht, Philip Ernst. PhD, Yale University, 1993.
"Tonal Stratification and Conflict in the Music of
Benjamin Britten."

253. Shelton, Margaret M. PhD, U. of Cal., Los Angeles, 1983.
"The ABC of 'Phaedra': Word Painting as
Structure in Britten's *Phaedra*."

254. Simons, H.R. DM, Indiana University, 1971.
"The Use of the Chorus in the Operas
of Benjamin Britten."

255. Smedley, Bruce R. PhD, Vanderbilt University, 1977.
"Contemporary Sacred Chamber Opera:
a Medieval Form in the Twentieth Century."

256. Snyder, Richard Dale. PhD, Indiana University, 1968.
"The Use of the Comic Idea in Selected Works of
Contemporary Opera (including *Albert Herring* and
A Midsummer Night's Dream by Britten.)

257. Stallings, Bonnie L. PhD, U. of Cal., Los Angeles, 1994.
"Diegetic Music in the Operas of Benjamin Britten:
The Case of *Peter Grimes*."

258. Stroeher, Vicki Pierce. PhD, North Texas State U., 1994.
"Form and Meaning in Benjamin Britten's
Sonnet Cycles."

259. Taggart, Mark Alan. DMA, Cornell University, 1983.
"Analysis of *Suite for Cello, Op. 72*
and *Second Suite for Cello, Op. 80.*"

260. Tibbets, George Richard. EdD, Columbia U., 1984.
"An Analysis of the Text-music Relationship
in Selected Songs of Benjamin Britten and
its Implications for the Interpretation of
His Solo Song Literature."

261. Tiemeyer, H.C. DMA, Catholic U. of America, 1977.
"An Analysis of *Third Suite for Cello Op. 87*
by Benjamin Britten."

262. Weber, Michael James. DMA, U. of Arizona, 1990.
"Benjamin Britten's *The Company of Heaven.*"

263. White, William Robert. DMA, U. of Texas, Austin, 1988.
"A Performer's Analysis of *The Holy Sonnets of
John Donne* by Benjamin Britten."

264. Whitesell, Lloyd Ashley, III. PhD, State University of
New York at Stony Brook, 1993.
"Images of Self in the Music of Benjamin Britten."

265. Whitmire, Mark Alexander. DMA, U. of Maryland, 1991.
"Songs by John Ireland and Benjamin Britten
to Poems by Thomas Hardy."

266. Winter, Jerome Lynn. DMA, University of Iowa, 1990.
"An Analysis and Perspective of *"Noye's Fludde"*
by Benjamin Britten."

The index includes references to all authors and contributors to the bibliography, identified directly (i.e., as the author of a principal text) or indirectly (i.e., as the contributor of an article or other item noted in a subordinate position to the cited text). Citations are referenced to entry numbers.